words t

may they be blessed

Book I | Psalms 1-50

written by
Makenzie Halbert-Howen & Ken Kuhn

May They Be Blessed
Book I | Psalms 1-50

Copyright © 2020 by Ken Kuhn, Makenzie Halbert-Howen

ALL RIGHTS RESERVED
No part of this publication may be reproduced, stored in a retrieval system, or transmitted in any form by any means—electronic, mechanical, photocopying, recording, or otherwise—without prior written consent.

All Scripture quotations, unless otherwise indicated, are taken from New Revised Standard Version Bible, copyright © 1989 National Council of the Churches of Christ in the United States of America. Used by permission. All rights reserved worldwide.

Scripture quotations noted ESV are from The ESV® Bible (The Holy Bible, English Standard Version®), copyright © 2001 by Crossway, a publishing ministry of Good News Publishers. Used by permission. All rights reserved.

While any stories in this book are true, some names and identifying information may have been changed to protect the privacy of the individuals.

ISBN 978-1-63625-800-3 (print)
ISBN 978-1-63625-801-0 (digital)

Printed in the United States of America

Cover design: Ken Kuhn
Interior design: Ken Kuhn

Constant Source | www.theconstantsource.com

Contents

Introduction	5	Psalm 26	62
Psalm 1	12	Psalm 27	64
Psalm 2	14	Psalm 28	66
Psalm 3	16	Psalm 29	68
Psalm 4	18	Psalm 30	70
Psalm 5	20	Psalm 31	72
Psalm 6	22	Psalm 32	74
Psalm 7	24	Psalm 33	76
Psalm 8	26	Psalm 34	78
Psalm 9	28	Psalm 35	80
Psalm 10	30	Psalm 36	82
Psalm 11	32	Psalm 37	84
Psalm 12	34	Psalm 38	86
Psalm 13	36	Psalm 39	88
Psalm 14	38	Psalm 40	90
Psalm 15	40	Psalm 41	92
Psalm 16	42	Psalm 42	94
Psalm 17	44	Psalm 43	96
Psalm 18	46	Psalm 44	98
Psalm 19	48	Psalm 45	100
Psalm 20	50	Psalm 46	102
Psalm 21	52	Psalm 47	104
Psalm 22	54	Psalm 48	106
Psalm 23	56	Psalm 49	108
Psalm 24	58	Psalm 50	110
Psalm 25	60	Acknowledgments	113

Introduction

1 You who live in the shelter of the Most High, who abide in the shadow of the Almighty, 2 will say to the Lord, "My refuge and my fortress; my God, in whom I trust."

Psalm 91:1-2

Imagine walking up to an arched wooden door. You place your hand on its face and feel its soft, smooth grain. Its warmth draws you in, beckoning you to enter. Your heart skips a beat in anticipation and you reach to open the door, but there is no knob or handle, so you lift your hand to knock. Before your knuckles rap the wooden planks, you hear a voice: "Come in," it says, with both the gentleness of a cool breeze and the strength of the summer sun. The chamber door cracks open and you step through, your senses drinking in every detail. The room is small, but cozy. A fire crackles beneath the mantle across the room. Two oversized, lived-in leather armchairs face one another in front of the fire. A shared circular side table fills the space between the chairs and the hearth; on it sits a cool glass of water, a small potted olive tree, an embroidered handkerchief, and a magnifying glass. Next to the chair is a small stool.

You take another step forward and notice a faint aroma of

peppermint, cinnamon, and pine that instills both a sense of comfort and adventure. You don't see anyone in the room and yet a powerful presence envelops you. Finally, you receive an instruction, an invitation heard in your heart, "Rest and reflect, listen and lament, feel joy and find hope. Come and just be with Me. Dwell."

At the very heart of Scripture is an invitation to a relationship with God. A relationship that defines the Christian's identity as a beloved child of God, that inspires us to live like Jesus and watch carefully for and join in the work of the Holy Spirit all around us. The book of Psalms poetically encourages us to experience God and allow that transformation to change the way we encounter the world. When God is our starting place, we begin to see the world, love others, and go about our humble tasks differently because we see them through the eyes of their Creator.

But how? How do we learn the heart of God? How do we allow our God-given identity to soak into the very core of our being? How do we help our unique and beautiful identity to animate our doing? And maybe most importantly, how do we share that way of life with our kids?

The answer, at least in part, can be found In the words of Psalm 91. In order to understand who God created us to be and how that impacts our every day, we must live, abide, and take refuge in the shelter of the Most High. In other words, we must learn to "dwell." I love that word, because as a noun it refers to a literal home or a place to live, and as a verb it means to take up residence and put down roots. Our home tends to be our safe place, the space to which we long to return whether the day has been difficult or a wonderful adventure. Our home is a place to rest, learn, love, and grow. Psalm 91 tells us that in order to fully absorb God, we must rest in, learn from, give and receive love, and abide in God. We must dwell.

The goal of this book is simply to help you and your child build a rhythm of consistently dwelling with God.

Like all healthy habits, God-focused practices, or faith rhythms

Introduction

as I like to call them, take time, energy, and repetition. When it comes to creating new habits, we know that the earlier one starts a new habit, the easier it is to stick with it. This is why we built this devotional tool with new parents and parents of preschoolers in mind. There is no better time to begin teaching your children about God, allowing God's truths to form their identity, and to set up faith rhythms that will guide them in their transformational journey with Jesus, than the early time in their lives when they are naturally establishing routines and rhythms.

Our little ones are already learning language, so it's a perfect opportunity to teach them the language of God. They are just beginning to learn morning routines. What if they grew up always associating breakfast time with Bible time? Or expected to receive an encouraging biblical truth before laying that sweet head down upon the pillow? We are already teaching them, through introduction and practice, to be emotionally and physically healthy little people. This is our opportunity to help them see from an early age that spiritual health is just as important if not more important than eating our veggies.

That being said, we know that early parenthood comes with its own set of challenges. We know how impossible it can feel to find a quiet moment for yourself. But, we also know that in order to flourish it is necessary to connect with God. In fact, it's because parenting is hard work that we are so passionate about creating space to rely on God to be at work in our lives and the lives of our kids. May They Be Blessed is designed to provide you with short meaningful moments to dwell with God that both help you to spiritually recharge and also give you the right words to speak the promises of God over your children.

There are so many different books and blogs that tell us how to parent. And even though we have the best intentions, we will always fall short, and it's for this very reason that we want to allow the voice of God and the words of Scripture to be a guiding light in our children's lives as soon as possible. The Bible promises us that, when we prioritize dwelling with God, we will flourish. When we seek God's way, it will be shown. And we believe that when our children see how God captures the hearts and brings delight to the lives of their parents, they too will know the love of God and it will be a natural thing for them to long for it too.

As parents, we have the beautiful opportunity to introduce our children to the wonder and awe of resting and reflecting, listening and lamenting, feeling joy, and finding hope in God. The invitation for us and for our children is simply to dwell.

The Power of Blessing

This little book is built around a long-standing biblical tradition: the blessing. Let's take a look at how the Bible defines blessing. One of the most commonly quoted blessings from the Bible is found in the Old Testament book of Numbers. In this portion of chapter 6, God is teaching Moses how the spiritual leaders of Israel–the priesthood–should bless God's people.

> "24 The Lord bless you
>   and keep you;
> 25 the Lord make his face shine on you
>   and be gracious to you;
> 26 the Lord turn his face toward you
>   and give you peace.
> Numbers 6:24-26

As teachers of God's people, the priesthood proclaimed blessings like the one from Numbers 6 to encourage, empower, and intercede–pray on behalf of–God's people. This alone should be enough of a reason for us to incorporate blessings into our parenting routines. But blessing also provides another layer of benefit: communicating the character of God. Blessings teach us something about who God is and who we are, they remind us that God is at work, and they invite us into deeper relationship with God and others. The blessing from Numbers 6 is a beautiful prayer of provision and peace that declares that God is at work, that God sees you personally, and that God is our source of grace and peace.

In short, blessings are concise, yet powerful statements that allow us to pray biblical truth over others, reveal and seek the character of God, and partner with them in asking God to be at work in our lives.

To this end, blessings are great teaching tools because they are short enough to memorize and repeat, but packed with truth. While researching in preparation for this book, I read many different blessings found in the Bible and in other Christian literature and noticed that the most powerful blessings were made up of a few key elements.

The foundation for a blessing that both affirms and instructs should first declare a truth about God's character that the recipient can internalize. Second, it may include an invitation for the recipient to experience God or the world in a new way. This can be in the form of asking God to make something clear, make the presence of the Holy Spirit known, or may even be an invitation to see the world differently. Finally, a blessing may encourage the recipient to embody the truth. This is the active response to the truth we learn about God. As one of my seminary professors liked to remind us, the way we think about God must influence the way we live in the world. So, a good blessing empowers the recipient to reflect Jesus in every aspect of life.

When it came to writing many of the blessings in this book, we combined the above elements into the following formula:

Blessing = May you (internalize + experience + embody)

As you grow more comfortable and familiar with blessings, I

encourage you to explore writing your own blessings to pray over your kids. Blessings provide an unparalleled opportunity for parents to begin to shape the narrative of God's immense love and instill foundational truths that proclaim who God is with their kids.

How to Use This Book

As we noted above, but it truly can't be overstated, parenting infants and toddlers makes for a very full and exhausting schedule. So, when we were dreaming up a format for this book we wanted to create a tool that helped new parents and parents of small children feel successful in establishing faith rhythms without feeling overwhelmed, which for us meant creating a resource that leads to spiritual growth for parents and provides a way to interact and share God with kids, but also is flexible enough to be used at whatever pace is best for your family.

To that end, May They Be Blessed is not a daily devotional. It is intentionally constructed to fit into whatever little space of time you have (this may be weekly or bi-weekly) for a devotional moment that reconnects you with God and gives you some things to ponder until the next time you pick it up.

Four sections are repeated through all fifty devotions. The first is Scripture. Each devotion is rooted in a passage of Scripture from the book of Psalms, which is found in the Old Testament of the Bible, and includes a snippet of the passage that gives context and provides the foundation for the biblical truth that is explored in section two. If you are a parent of older kids and/or have a little bit of extra time, we encourage you to dive into each of these devotions with your Bible in hand and read the entire Psalm.

The second section, entitled "Truth," presents a short commentary on what the Scripture passage says about God and how we should interpret and begin to apply that information in our lives.

The third section contains a blessing that incorporates parts of

Introduction

the Truth section into a prayer that you can read out loud over your children. A good time for this is when you are holding them or have a quiet moment to reach out, touch them, and proclaim gently the goodness of God.

The fourth section provides a reflection question. Reading and interpreting Scripture are great ways to learn and experience God, but in reflection, we process who God is and how our lives are different because of our relationship with Jesus Christ.

In summary, sections one and two highlight and unpack a characteristic of God found in the psalms. Section three provides a blessing to help you share that truth with your kids and section four helps you consider and apply what you are learning about God's character. We recommend that as you make your way through each devotion you allow the reflection questions to bounce around in your brain as you go about your day and that you pray the blessing aloud over your children multiple times. In fact, if along the way you find a blessing that is especially meaningful to you, keep proclaiming it over your children for as long as it continues to powerfully elicit a response in your heart.

Remember that in every part of this devotional experience the Holy Spirit is present and at work in the Word of God, in the pondering of your heart, and the blessings you bestow.

> May you be a family that dwells deeply in the Lord, may you experience God's wonder and love, and may it transform you into people who share that love with the world.

Psalm 1

1 Happy are those
 who do not follow the advice of the wicked,
 or take the path that sinners tread,
 or sit in the seat of scoffers;

2 but their delight is in the law of the Lord,
 and on his law they meditate day and night.

3 They are like trees
 planted by streams of water,
 which yield their fruit in its season,
 and their leaves do not wither.
 In all that they do, they prosper.

Truth

The book of Psalms opens with the wise psalmist explaining the importance of a life lived in connection with God. The image of the tree that the psalmist uses in 1:3 reminds us that God is our source of life. The promise found in Psalm 1 is that if we rely on God, take the time to soak in the words of the Lord, and consistently pursue a relationship with Jesus, we will flourish.

The illustration of the tree is encouraging because it reminds us of the ways that God is carefully and intentionally tending to those who abide in Christ. The phrase "planted by streams of water" reminds us that we have been purposefully placed and given the resources we need. The phrase "yield their fruit in its season " reminds us that there are high points and low points along the journey, but the promise is fruitfulness. When we are rooted in Christ, we will be people that are identified by the way we look like him. The phrase "their roots do not wither " encourages us that even in the barren seasons, we can continue on, knowing that the God we serve promises new life. Finally, this portion of the Psalm ends with the promise of flourishing. In all we do, God will go with us.

The bottom-line truth is that God is irrevocably and unquestioningly for us. God desires for us to be in a rhythm of a relationship that prioritizes a life spent in connection with the Creator, which ultimately becomes our lifeline, the sustenance we need to engage and thrive in each new day. Blessed are those who delight in the Lord. Today's truth is that when we abide in Christ, we will flourish.

Blessing

May you be like a tree that draws deeply from God, the stream of life. May God help you to see that you have been planted on purpose. May you draw your strength from your creator, may you live in the promise that God will be with you in every season, and may you flourish in every stage of growth. Amen.

Reflection

How are you encouraged by who God is today?

Psalm 2

4 He who sits in the heavens laughs;
  the Lord has them in derision.

5 Then he will speak to them in his wrath,
  and terrify them in his fury, saying,

6 "I have set my king on Zion, my holy hill."

12 kiss his feet,
  or he will be angry, and you will perish in the way;
  for his wrath is quickly kindled.

  Happy are all who take refuge in him.

Truth

Sometimes the world, at large, can seem a bit bleak. With global information at our fingertips every minute of the day, it's easy to get pulled down by the evil of our world: corrupt leaders, famine, war, disease. When the state of the world feels overwhelming to me, I remember and am thankful that I have a hope that holds strong beyond the days of my own finite time on earth.

This is the truth of this psalm that still rings true today. Jesus Christ, the Messiah, is seated on high, on God's holy mountain, sovereign over the rulers of the earth. Though it is true that God is a God who comforts and draws near to us in our darkest moments, God is also a God who fights for us. God is more powerful than any enemy we might face on earth. God transcends earthly power and the Kingdom of God will one day fully rule on earth.

To me, that is a great comfort, to know that our heartbreak, our sadness, our defeat on earth doesn't go unrecognized, and God, our

God of justice, brings fury and wrath against iniquity in the world and provides refuge for God's people.

Blessing

May you be confident in the Lord's strength. May you rest in a power and a hope that is greater than anything we may face on earth. May you seek refuge in the mighty arms of God, drawing near to the one is who is powerful above all else.

Reflection

How does the truth of God's wrath and might affect the way you see the world?

May They Be Blessed

Psalm 3

---

*1 O Lord, how many are my foes!
   Many are rising against me;*

*2 many are saying to me,
   "There is no help for you in God."*

*3 But you, O Lord, are a shield around me,
   my glory, and the one who lifts up my head.*

*4 I cry aloud to the Lord,
   and he answers me from his holy hill.*

*5 I lie down and sleep;
   I wake again, for the Lord sustains me.*

*6 I am not afraid of ten thousands of people
   who have set themselves against me all
       around.*

*7 Rise up, O Lord!
   Deliver me, O my God!
  For you strike all my enemies on the cheek;
   you break the teeth of the wicked.*

*8 Deliverance belongs to the Lord;
   may your blessing be on your people!*

Truth

Have you felt overwhelmed lately? Like one negative experience led to another and another and you find yourself asking how many things can go wrong. Or maybe there just seems to be way too much to do. Do you find the time to accomplish one task just to find three more things rising up needing to be done? David wrote this psalm, and that is how he was feeling. Completely overwhelmed by the adversity that comes with running a kingdom, he turns to God for strength. You see, David knows a few things about God that would benefit us as well. He knows that God hears us, sustains us, and delivers us in our times of need.

In verse 3, David cries out because he knows God is listening and will answer. In verse 4, he is able to find rest because he knows that in the face of overwhelming odds it is ultimately God who gives us the strength to make it through. Finally, in verse 7, David calls upon the Lord to deliver him. He does this because he knows (verse 8) that our God is a God of deliverance. When we look at the story of Jesus Christ in the New Testament, deliverance is a fundamental characteristic of God that led God to dwell with us. The bottom-line truth is that God will see us through. Be encouraged that in the face of to-do lists that are too long and needs that are hard to meet, God is there to see us through.

Blessing

Little one, rest well knowing that the God of the universe sustains you. When things are hard, boldly cry out knowing that the God of all people hears you and will answer you. And when you find yourself in a space not knowing which way to go, may you find hope in Jesus Christ the author of deliverance and the giver of strength. Amen.

Reflection

How is God bringing you rest today?

Psalm 4

3 But know that the Lord has set apart the faithful for himself; the Lord hears when I call to him.

*7 You have put gladness in my heart
more than when their grain and wine abound.*

*8 I will both lie down and sleep in peace;
for you alone, O Lord, make me lie down in safety.*

Truth

Perhaps it is because I am a parent, a nurturer, and a caretaker, but I feel most connected to God when I read and meditate on God's gentleness. God listens, God hears, God protects, God provides peace. Yes, God fights and brings wrath, but Scripture tells us again and again, like the Psalmist, that God hears us.

It is at times perplexing to think of a God who sits high above the affairs of earth, enacting a will and a plan for a coming Kingdom that is unfathomable to us on earth, our lifetime but a blip on the radar. God is big. This is a comfort, of course, but I find myself at peace when I dwell on the truth that God is also here, with us, right now. God is the orchestrator of all of history, but God and the Spirit of God dwell with me, in my life, in my days of to-do lists, chores, and caring for tiny people. God is there. God is there in my victories, in my heartbreak, and in my days ahead. God hears me.

To rest in the truth of the Creator of the universe hearing our calls is enough, but that is not all we know to be true of God. God is an active participator in the relationship with us. The psalmist tells us that God puts gladness in our hearts. No matter the state of the world, our lives, or our circumstances, God has given us gladness, peace, joy because God cares for us deeply. God alone creates for us true safety, new hope, and joy in the morning. God is our ultimate nurturer. God is with us.

Blessing

May you know the true gladness of the Creator. May you rest and grow and flourish in the truth that God knows all of you and hears your cries. May you know peace as you draw more near to God who cares for you and sustains you and walks with you every day.

Reflection

Do you rely on God as if you truly believe God will hear you? How might that shift in perspective alter your relationship to God?

Psalm 5

*7 But I, through the abundance of your steadfast love,
will enter your house,*

*I will bow down toward your holy temple
in awe of you.*

*8 Lead me, O Lord, in your righteousness
because of my enemies;
make your way straight before me.*

Truth

The God we serve is a God of abundance. The promise of abundance is woven throughout scripture. There is the story in 1 Kings 17 of the widow who used her last handful of flour and final drops of oil to bake bread for Elijah, which no matter how much bread she made, never ran out. This story reminds us that our God is a God of unending resources. In the gospels, Jesus, God in the flesh, washes the feet of the disciples, heals the sick, befriends the outcast, and empowers the marginalized voices of His culture. In Jesus, we see God abundantly caring for creation. And circling back to Psalm 5, the psalmist reminds us that the abundance he has experienced is in the form of love. God loves us abundantly. God loves you abundantly and God loves your child abundantly without end.

In a culture that seeks opulent materialism but often experiences isolation and relational scarcity, the abundance of God is one of the most encouraging characteristics of God. Especially when we realize as the psalmist has in verses 7b and 8, that God's abundance is invitational. God desires to be in a relationship with us because God abundantly loves us. We are invited to turn to God in the hard moments, in the face of adversity, and the times where we don't know the right answer. Sometimes navigating relationships with our spouses, infants, friends, or even God can seem hard, but it's in those moments that we can rest in God's abundant love, care, and provision for us because we know that God's abundant love is working through us in the lives of those for which we care so deeply. So if today you find yourself tired and lonely, whole and happy, or somewhere in between, rest in God's abundance.

Blessing

I pray that you would know God's abundance and that you would profoundly experience it throughout your life. May you know the depths of love, the width of forgiveness, the immensity of grace, and the steadfast, unending provision that God has for you. May we be instruments of that abundance in your life and may you become an agent of abundance to those you meet along the way.

Reflection

Where have you experienced God's abundance and how do you need to experience it today?

Psalm 6

4 Turn, O Lord, save my life;
  deliver me for the sake of your steadfast love.

5 For in death there is no remembrance of you;
  in Sheol who can give you praise?

6 I am weary with my moaning;
  every night I flood my bed with tears;
  I drench my couch with my weeping.

7 My eyes waste away because of grief;
  they grow weak because of all my foes.

Truth

There is freedom to be found in meditating on the words of lament found in Scripture. So often, especially for those of us who were raised in the Christian church, we are told to be truly glad, to be joyful in all things, because we were saved. We were sinners, unworthy of forgiveness, yet God sent Christ to atone for our sins, to save us. And this is amazing! We should rejoice in this! But for too long, I let this truth weigh on me. Who was I to cry out to God in anguish, to lament the pain of my life, to be angry at a God who allows for sin and death and disease? For too long, I felt that I wasn't allowed to cry out to God in anger or grief because it would mean appearing ungrateful for all that God had given me.

But this is not the attitude that we see in Scripture. We see broken and sinful people, like David, the author of this Psalm, who at times are faithful and admirable, but who at other times are desperate, grief-stricken, and without hope. In fact, crying out to God in despair, lamenting, is extremely biblical. There's an entire book about it! When I read these passages, that speak plainly of the pain of human existence, but are tinged with a hope that can only exist with God, I feel myself breathe a sigh of relief. It is not sinful or ungrateful to bring all of our emotions—yes, even anger—before God. What kind of relationship can exist if I only come to God with thanksgiving and gladness? It would be shallow and disingenuine.

David pleads with God to save his life in this psalm, so that he may continue to live a life of praise. But even though David was called to a great purpose, he does not demand that God save his life. He doesn't say, "I deserve this!" or "You owe me!" David pleads with a God whose ways are far beyond his own to save him, so that he may continue to do his work in the world. But we don't know God's plans, and God's will is at times painful and confusing to us, and that is why lament is so necessary for our Christian lives.

Blessing

May you come boldly before God in all seasons. May you seek God's comfort and hand in times of sadness and in times of great joy. May you rest in knowing that God has given you a great purpose on earth and hears your cries.

Reflection

Do you come to God in times of despair as well as times of thanksgiving? Do you allow yourself to be stripped bare, in all of your humanness, before God?

Psalm 7

8 The Lord judges the peoples;
judge me, O Lord, according to my righteousness
and according to the integrity that is in me.

9 O let the evil of the wicked come to an end,
but establish the righteous,
you who test the minds and hearts,
O righteous God.

Truth

When I read verse 8, depending on the day, my response to the psalmist's invitation for God to judge him according to his righteousness varies widely. Some days I couldn't agree more, I feel like my circumstances aren't lining up with the work that I've put in and I wish that I could get a little bit of credit. Other days, this idea is terrifying because I know that I am an imperfect person who deserves way worse than the abundance of blessings that I have been given. Yet, the beautiful part about Psalm 7 is that there is encouragement no matter where you find yourself today.

For those of us looking for a little bit of recognition, we can find hope in the truth that God is watching. Jesus says in His parable found in Matthew 25:40, "Truly I tell you, just as you did it to one of the least of these who are members of my family, you did it to me." When we act in integrity, seek Christ, and care for those around us, God receives it as worship. The psalmist says in verse 9 that the Lord is the one who sees and tests our minds and hearts. May He find them looking more and more like Jesus.

At other times the word "test" can give us a sinking feeling in our chests. Maybe we've recently fallen back into an old habit for comfort during these trying times or maybe the extraordinary stress of life with a new baby is revealing deep-seated selfishness that we didn't realize was present. No matter the reason, when we read these words we are disheartened by the truth that our sin is seen. Here's the encouragement for us today: God is a God of incalculable and unimaginable grace. God knows you intimately. God knows where you are, the season you are in, and the person you are becoming. The Holy Spirit is animating the good parts of your life and the blood of Jesus has washed the bad parts away.

No matter where you are today, know that God sees you, knows your heart and mind, and loves you abundantly.

Blessing

As you grow, may you believe that you are known intimately by God and those around you. When you feel underappreciated may you know that even when the people around you don't see your actions, God does, and receives them as worship. And in the hard times, when the world seems to be winning, may you know the abundant love of Christ and that the almighty God of the universe sees past your sin and straight to your heart and your mind.

Reflection

Do you need recognition today, or do you need to experience grace? Ask God in prayer to encourage your soul to that end today.

Psalm 8

*3 When I look at your heavens, the work of your fingers,
the moon and the stars that you have established;*

*4 what are human beings that you are mindful of them,
mortals that you care for them?*

*5 Yet you have made them a little lower than God,
and crowned them with glory and honor.*

*6 You have given them dominion over the works of your hands;
you have put all things under their feet,*

Truth

I love the way the psalmist chooses to phrase this passage. The admission of all that God is capable of, the awe-inspiring work of creation is enough to leave us speechless. It's a recognition that God, the Creator of the universe, has no need to be concerned with human affairs. What are we to God? Especially when we consider the context in which the psalmist was writing, the gods of other religions were angry and wrathful and gave little thought to the people who served them, apart from demanding sacrifice and worship. And though we see the God of the Bible bring wrath upon sinful people, we also see that same God elevate humans beyond what we deserve. God created all things, and yet God chooses us to care for that creation. Why even include us in the equation?

I've encountered too many people who view the God of the Old Testament as a vengeful and angry God, while characterizing Jesus as the loving, forgiving Son of God. But the truth is, God, and Jesus and the Spirit, though distinct, are one. It's the paradox of the triune God, a God who is relational even in being. God is all-powerful, yet God loves people in tangible and tender ways, charging us to advocate for creation, crowning us with glory and honor. And Jesus reflects both of these parts of God. The Christian God, the multi-faceted, all-powerful God, is relational by nature. This is what sets the triune God apart from other religions. Scripture tells us that we are sinners in need of a savior, but it doesn't stop there. Despite the tragedy of the human condition, our God still elevates us, grafting us into a holy family, and trusts us with creation. Our God is mindful of us, despite all of the ways that we prove ourselves unworthy.

Blessing

May you remember that you are treasured and loved by a loving God, put on earth for a purpose. May you care for the things with which you've been entrusted and strive to see the image of God reflected in everyone around you and yourself, resting in the truth that God sees us, hears us, and is mindful of us.

Reflection

How often do you stop to think about the multi-faceted nature of God? How does it change your relationship to know that God is simultaneously above us yet involved in our lives?

Psalm 9

*1 I will give thanks to the Lord with my whole heart;
I will tell of all your wonderful deeds.*

*2 I will be glad and exult in you;
I will sing praise to your name, O Most High.*

Truth

When I was a child, my parents had some financially difficult times. During one of those times their car, the one that got us back and forth from school and extracurricular activities, broke down beyond repair or at least the repairs would have cost more than the vehicle was worth. So, with a meager down payment in hand, we all went car shopping. We shopped for hours, driving between different car dealerships, sitting and test driving multiple cars, and then we found it. The perfect car. It checked all of the boxes except one. It was just a bit too expensive. The down payment that my parents had pulled together just wasn't quite enough. They knew they could afford the car in another month, but they doubted this car would still be available. And so, we returned home bummed out and still one car down from what we needed.

When we got home my mom went out to get the mail and ran back exclaiming that God had given us the money we needed to get the car. While I can't remember what the source of the money was, that's not the point, because, in fact, it didn't matter. What mattered was my parents' response, which was that this mystery check, the money we needed for a car, came from God. Now as adults we can probably explain away the origins of the check. But the point is that I will never forget the overwhelming gratitude that they felt at that moment and the fact that they told everyone that their new-to-them car was a gift from God. The moral of the story is that when we share in God's wonder with our kids, they remember it for their whole life.

When the psalmist pledges to tell of all of God's wonderful deeds, he is promising to testify to the ways that God has infiltrated, changed, and made his life better in every way. We will see this again and again throughout the Psalms because it is an integral facet of this book. Sharing what God has done in the life of the Church and its members has been and will always be one of the most encouraging parts about being a part of God's family.

Blessing

May stories of the wonderful deeds of the Lord always find their way to your ears. May you grow up sharing your experiences with others and in all things may you seek and find the ways in which God is at work. I pray that my voice will be one that constantly tells of God's grandeur and that together we may always stand in awe of God's wonder.

Reflection

What stories of God's goodness can you begin sharing with your child now, even if they won't remember?

Psalm 10

1 Why, O Lord, do you stand far off?
  Why do you hide yourself in times of trouble?

2 In arrogance the wicked persecute the poor—
  let them be caught in the schemes they have devised...

14 But you do see! Indeed you note trouble and grief,
  that you may take it into your hands;
  the helpless commit themselves to you;
  you have been the helper of the orphan.

Truth

In this psalm, the psalmist cries out to God as he watches the most vulnerable people suffer under oppression. It is easy to understand the defeat and despair of his lament. In our modern world, we are subject to a 24-hour news cycle, the internet has made our world smaller than ever, and it seems as though we can't pick up our phones or turn on the TV without hearing about war, oppression, injustice, slavery, or genocide. The world is deeply broken, and when the most vulnerable people continue to suffer and die, it is difficult to feel that our sovereign God is near.

    The psalmist doesn't shy away from that, and the pain in these words is palpable. It is a horrible feeling to watch evil rulers win and God's people suffer, but we know that evil will not have the final word. Scripture tells us that God mourns with us; God sees our pain, and the eventual fulfillment of God's Kingdom will not let that suffering be in vain. Despite the greater promise, we still have to endure the injustices and brokenness of life on earth. Yet we also serve a compassionate God. God doesn't ask us to turn our faces away from injustice, to fix our eyes only on the coming Kingdom.

God calls us to partner in redemptive work while we're still on earth, to pay attention to hurting and vulnerable people and to cry out for deliverance, to bring justice. This is what the psalmist is doing in this passage. And despite the honest lament in most of the passage, the psalm ends with a declaration of who God is. God hears our trouble and will not ignore our pleas. God, who has been a helper to the orphan, will continue to deliver hurting people.

Blessing

May you draw near to God in times of trouble, asking for God's help, trusting in the Kingdom yet to come. May you never turn a blind eye to oppression or injustice, but instead, work to restore dignity in all of God's creation.

Reflection

Do you at times struggle with pervasive evil in our world? How can you be honest with God about feelings of despair while still drawing near to God in times of hardship?

Psalm 11

*1 In the Lord I take refuge; how can you say to me,
"Flee like a bird to the mountains;*

*2 for look, the wicked bend the bow,
they have fitted their arrow to the string,
to shoot in the dark at the upright in heart.*

*3 If the foundations are destroyed,
what can the righteous do?"*

*4 The Lord is in his holy temple;
the Lord's throne is in heaven.
His eyes behold, his gaze examines humankind.*

*7 For the Lord is righteous;
he loves righteous deeds;
the upright shall behold his face.*

Truth

The psalmist, most likely King David, has found himself in a tricky spot. He is in the midst of a really difficult decision and is caught in the tension between the advice of his counselors and the truth that he knows in his heart. Have you felt this before? While you may not have a literal army threatening your life, have you ever felt like an army of critics is watching and waiting to criticize your every move? I know I have, and it is to this end that the psalmist offers us encouragement today.

Starting with the second part of verse 1 and continuing through verse 3, the psalmist quotes the warning of his advisors who are saying 'run away because if you die, the foundations will crumble and we won't know what to do.' The psalmist's response to this warning is a question: 'How can you instruct me to run while our all-powerful Creator is still on the throne, still in power?' While the psalmist is relying on God's protection and feels confident in staying, it's important to realize that many other times in his life King David did flee. The question becomes how did he know which to do? The answer lies in the first and final lines of Psalm 11. The psalmist begins by saying that he takes refuge in the Lord. The imagery of refuge all throughout the Bible is so beautiful. Refuge language describes the loving, nurturing, and relational aspects of God. At the end of our passage, the psalmist closes by using a common metaphor for knowing God. When held together, we learn that the psalmist's secret is intimacy with God. In knowing God and God's will, the psalmist knows the decision that needs to be made.

Like King David, sometimes our critics will agree with us and sometimes they won't, but we can find encouragement and confidence in knowing that when we seek refuge in Christ God will give us wisdom and direction.

Blessing

May you seek refuge in the arms of your Creator and may you stand strong in your resolve when the voices around you oppose that which God has shared with you.

Reflection

In what ways is your confidence growing because of your intimacy with God?

Psalm 12

---

6 *The promises of the Lord are promises that are pure,*
  silver refined in a furnace on the ground,
  purified seven times.

7 *You, O Lord, will protect us;*
  you will guard us from this generation forever.

8 *On every side the wicked prowl,*
  as vileness is exalted among humankind.

Truth

Here the psalmist is asking for God's help to deliver him because no godly people remain. This feeling is not uncommon to us as Christians. Though the psalmist lived in another time and place, in a culture in which those who served God were persecuted by foreign nations, we can identify with the loneliness that the psalmist describes. Christianity has been counter-cultural from its inception. The God of the Bible and the teachings of Jesus constantly call us to serve others before ourselves, to seek righteousness over wealth, and to lay down our lives in pursuit of an eternal kingdom. It goes against our human nature, yet we were created and designed to reflect the image of a loving and self-giving God. Feeling isolated in pursuit of godly living can make the task of being godly seem even more insurmountable.

But as the psalmist declares in the closing lines of the psalm, God doesn't abandon us; God protects us. God will guard us against the sinful generations, even when it seems like humanity as a whole exalts vileness. Though the psalmist's world is much different than the world we live in, the character of God he describes is an age-old truth. Our God does not change, and God's timeless word is just as relevant and powerful today. Humanity will continue to fall short of God's glory, and evil people will continue to prowl, but God doesn't leave us abandoned, not then, and not now.

Blessing

May you draw near to our God who never changes, the keeper of promises and the deliverer of humanity. May you cry out to God in times of injustice, in times of loneliness, and in the face of pain. May you know the protective power of our unwavering God.

Reflection

Can you relate to the loneliness expressed by the psalmist? Do you seek the comfort and protection of God in times of distress and isolation?

Psalm 13

1 How long, O Lord? Will you forget me forever?
How long will you hide your face from me?

2 How long must I bear pain in my soul,
and have sorrow in my heart all day long?
How long shall my enemy be exalted over me?

5 But I trusted in your steadfast love;
my heart shall rejoice in your salvation.

6 I will sing to the Lord,
because he has dealt bountifully with me.

Truth

Sometimes living in this fallen world can be really hard. It can be isolating, lonely, cold, and painful. Have you ever cried out a question like the psalmist is asking here? Have you muttered it under your breath or screamed it out loud in an empty room? I have. When I was twenty-one years old, one of my closest friends in the world died from cancer. I will never forget the emptiness and sorrow that I felt in that season. I would open my mouth to ask God why she was gone or why I couldn't even feel God's presence, but my breath would catch in my chest and I'd just weep. I felt that pain deep in my soul and even writing that now, a tinge of it still exists. This life is filled with unfathomable lows, but the truth is that God is always with us. Even when God's face seems to be nowhere to be seen, the truth is that God is weeping too. We know that's true because we see it in Jesus. The shortest verse in the New Testament tells us as much, "Jesus wept" (John 11:35). This was Jesus's response to the death of His friend, but in this moment we also see the way that God interacts with the brokenness of the world and the rich involvement that God has in creation.

What I love about Psalm 13 is that it doesn't resolve. Nowhere in Psalm 13 does the psalmist hear from God or see an immediate result. Instead, at the end of the psalm, the psalmist reflects on the truth that God is, has been, and will always be with us even when we can't see God's face. It's a reminder that in the truly dark days, when there isn't a resolution in sight, that God's faithfulness is our hope. Know still that God deals bountifully with each of us.

Blessing

Little one, the world is a hard place to live sometimes. And, as much as it pains me to say it, you will encounter hardship in your life. I pray that when you do that you will remember that you are steadfastly loved. I pray that the distance you feel between you and God passes quickly and that God's abundance resonates in all parts of your life.

Reflection

How has God dealt bountifully with you in the past? Is there darkness that needs resolution? Lift that up to God in prayer.

Psalm 14

5 There they shall be in great terror,
   for God is with the company of the righteous.

6 You would confound the plans of the poor,
   but the Lord is their refuge.

7 O that deliverance for Israel would come from Zion!
   When the Lord restores the fortunes of his people,
   Jacob will rejoice; Israel will be glad.

Truth

A repeated idea, both in the psalms and throughout all of scripture, is that God is a God who cares for the poor. The Lord is a refuge for the poor, but what does "the poor" mean in the context of the time when the psalmist was writing? In our modern culture, we often think of the poor as being people with very little money or material wealth. But in the ancient culture in which the books of scripture were written, "the poor" refers to those of low social class, social outcasts, or the oppressed. Jesus speaks of the poor often, and the book of Luke repeats the theme of Jesus' Kingdom being, "good news for the poor" (Luke 4:18, Luke 6:20, 7:22, 14:13). Through Jesus' teachings, he makes clear that some of the social outcasts included in this definition sometimes had material wealth, like tax collectors, who were hated by many in their community.

So what does it mean that God elevates and protects the poor? It boils down to where God places value. Counter to our own culture, God doesn't place value on material wealth, or power, or prestige, or anything like that. God seeks out the most vulnerable, the ones that society deems unworthy, and God provides refuge for these people. The least of society are elevated before God. And beyond providing safety for these people, God will also restore the fortunes of these people. In God's Kingdom, the last shall be first. And as followers of God, we too should seek to elevate, protect, and dignify the ones that society deems less powerful, less important, or "poor." We should reject the allure of earthly wealth and the constant drive for power and instead be a people who, like our God, are protectors of the poor.

Blessing

May you seek what is right in all things. May you seek the well-being and care of all of God's people before selfish gain, power, and wealth. May you reflect the goodness of God and see God's image in all people.

Reflection

How do you protect "the poor" in your community? How might you reflect God more in the way you serve and treat the people around you?

Psalm 15

1 O Lord, who may abide in your tent?
Who may dwell on your holy hill?

2 Those who walk blamelessly, and do what is right,
and speak the truth from their heart;

3 who do not slander with their tongue,
and do no evil to their friends,
nor take up a reproach against their neighbors;

4 in whose eyes the wicked are despised,
but who honor those who fear the Lord;
who stand by their oath even to their hurt;

5 who do not lend money at interest,
and do not take a bribe against the innocent.
Those who do these things shall never be moved.

Truth

In Psalm 15, we see what it means to be a person who is becoming more like Christ. In verse 1, the psalmist tees up this theme by asking "who may abide in your tent?" With this question, the psalmist is asking, what does a person who belongs to the community of God look like?

In verse 2, the psalmist begins to describe the importance of walking blamelessly, doing justice, and speaking truth. As verse 2 flows into verse 3, the psalmist discusses the ways that the words from our mouths impact those around us. The psalmist encourages us to speak truth not slander, to empower our friends instead of tearing them down, and to love our neighbors instead of treating them with reproach. Verse 4 encourages the reader to stand up for Christian virtues, no matter the social repercussions that may result.

Finally, in verse 5, the psalmist instructs us to not charge interest on the money we loan others. To be clear, this isn't a critique of modern financial business practices, but rather a critique on the character of the loaner. If someone is in need, then do as Christ did and give without expecting anything in return, and especially do not treat the innocent with treachery.

In short, when the psalmist meditates on the word of the Lord and on the character of God, the psalmist concludes that those who belong in the community of God are focused on acting justly towards others. When we sit with the challenges presented here and allow the Holy Spirit to change our hearts, our actions begin to fall in line with the heart of God.

Blessing

May you experience the joys of participating in the community of God. May you seek justice in all you do, may you speak truthfully out of love, and as you grow, may your heart look more and more like the heart of God.

Reflection

How are you practicing some of these virtues as you become more like Christ?

Psalm 16

5 The Lord is my chosen portion and my cup;
*   you hold my lot.*

6 The lines have fallen for me in pleasant places;
*   indeed, I have a beautiful inheritance.*

7 I bless the Lord who gives me counsel;
*   in the night also my heart instructs me.*

8 I have set the Lord always before me;
*   because he is at my right hand, I shall not be shaken.*

(English Standard Version)

Truth

I absolutely love Psalm 16. I think David does a beautiful job of capturing the unique peace that comes with belonging to God in faith. Though David speaks of the blessings bestowed on those who put their faith in God, we know from David's other writings and the story of his life that he had no easy path. Though there is peace of mind and hope offered to those who trust in God, there is no guarantee of an easy life. But no matter what David encounters in life, he knows that God is in control; God holds his lot. And beyond the ways that God directs our paths and cares for us, God also promises an inheritance, an eternal joy, for those who put their trust in God.

David also speaks of the Lord's counsel to him, the ways that his heart instructs him. As followers of God, we are not left to fend for ourselves throughout the trials and heartbreak of life on earth. We have a direct line to the Creator God, a relationship where we can seek counsel as well as comfort and refuge. David knew God intimately, and today, we can have this same relationship through the revelation of Scripture and the work of Christ. And we too can have the truth of who God is etched in our hearts to instruct us in our lives even when we don't have the words to cry out in prayer. What a beautiful truth to know that no matter what we may face, we have the strength and wisdom of God to draw from. We cannot be shaken.

Blessing

May you find security and hope in the promises of God. May you seek the strength and comfort of God in times of weakness and fear. May you know of your inheritance and the true gift that comes with faith in the Creator God.

Reflection

Have you taken the time recently to rest in the promise of God's inheritance? Do you allow yourself to take refuge in the Creator?

Psalm 17

2 From you let my vindication come;
let your eyes see the right.

3 If you try my heart, if you visit me by night,
if you test me, you will find no wickedness in me;
my mouth does not transgress.

4 As for what others do, by the word of your lips
I have avoided the ways of the violent.

5 My steps have held fast to your paths;
my feet have not slipped.

6 I call upon you, for you will answer me, O God;
incline your ear to me, hear my words.

7 Wondrously show your steadfast love,
O savior of those who seek refuge
from their adversaries at your right hand.

Truth

Psalm 17 paints the picture of a person who has stayed up all night petitioning the Lord for deliverance and ends up being filled with hope. As we've seen in the Psalms before, the psalmist is confident that the way in which he has lived his life has been pleasing to God, yet the phrasing in this particular Psalm elicits an encouraging Biblical truth that deserves our attention today.

In verses 3 and 4, the psalmist, King David, is attempting to justify what he is asking for by his own goodness and behavior. In other words, the psalmist believes that he deserves to be saved because he is a good person. If you know King David's story you know that quite a few of his actions were less than pure. And yet,

David's story shows that God hears him and extends "wonderous and steadfast love" to him. Why? Because God's love for David and for us isn't contingent on our actions, our words, our feelings, or our thoughts. God just simply loves us.

In verse 3, David says that upon searching his life that the Lord would find no wickedness. Now even though David thinks this is because he has followed the right path and said the right thing, it isn't. Yet, it is still true that we are truly seen as cleansed, unblemished by the wickedness we've committed in our lives. The Bible gives us two reasons for this. First, Jesus advocates on our behalf at the right hand of God, and the Holy Spirit is at work in our lives. Second, following Jesus is a posture of the heart. So, in trying David's heart, the Lord sees a person who is honestly seeking after God.

In short, Psalm 17 is encouraging because whether we have blown it, or whether we believe we are righteous, God hears us, God loves us, and God has delivered us through Jesus. When we are searched, we are seen as clean not because we've earned it but because it's been freely given.

Blessing

May you know that you don't have to seek God's approval or love, but that it has already been given ten thousand times over. Yet, may your heart yearn to be obedient to the movement of the Spirit in your life, and may you know that God hears you and walks with you at all times.

Reflection

Rest and reflect in the truth that you are covered and advocated for by the son of God, Jesus Christ.

Psalm 18

---

1 I love you, O Lord, my strength.

2 The Lord is my rock, my fortress, and my deliverer,
my God, my rock in whom I take refuge,
my shield, and the horn of my salvation, my stronghold.

3 I call upon the Lord, who is worthy to be praised,
so I shall be saved from my enemies.

Truth

This psalm is incredibly dense and quite lengthy. There is much to meditate on and draw upon here, but I love the familiarity of the first few lines, which brings to mind hymns and songs sung in Christian churches for generations. I've sung these words more times than I can count. "The Lord is my strength, the Lord is my rock. I call upon the Lord who is worthy to be praised." But when I pause, when I read through these words carefully and meditate on the many verses that follow, I realize the majesty and power present in these words that had been diluted over time by my own familiarity with them. These aren't simple words to make us feel good when we sing them, they're a declaration of God's strength and power over the most brutal of earthly forces.

David goes on for many verses, illustrating an impressive show of strength from God, showing exactly what God is capable of: mountains quaking, darkness cloaking, the foundations of the earth laid bare at the rebuke of our mighty God. Not only is God the ultimate stronghold in a raging war, but God also controls the earth, light, darkness, wind, and waves. David uses metaphor and rich poetry to show that nothing, absolutely nothing, on earth is bigger than God. I think I've sung these words too many times without taking the time to dwell on the majesty of all that God is. And though God is mighty beyond what we can imagine, David trusts in Him for deliverance. He cries out to God. I love verse 16, where David says, "He reached down from on high, and he took hold of me. (NIV)" The almighty and transcendent God reaches down and saves us.

Blessing

May you always have faith in the deliverance of God. May you be in awe of God's strength and know that God is bigger than any earthly force or anything you will ever face. May you trust in the unshakeable fortress and refuge of our God.

Reflection

When was the last time you sat in awe of God? Look around you, what leaves you awestruck? Say a quick prayer of thanks in response to all that God is doing in the midst of the place and time in which you find yourself.

Psalm 19

---

1 The heavens are telling the glory of God;
and the firmament proclaims his handiwork.

2 Day to day pours forth speech,
and night to night declares knowledge.

3 There is no speech, nor are there words;
their voice is not heard;

4 yet their voice goes out through all the earth,
and their words to the end of the world.

Truth

When was the last time that you stopped to smell the roses–literally? When you are driving down a tree-lined street in the early autumn, what thoughts cross your mind? How about the feel of the sand on your feet at the beach, and the vastness of the body of water that lies before you–does this remind you of God? The truth found in Psalm 19 is simple, the world's grandeur testifies to God's glory and its beauty to the Creator's design.

In this psalm, the author is caught up in the powerful testimony that the world proclaims about God. The psalmist personifies night and day, noting that they both communicate and teach us about God. The turning of the seasons reminds us that there is a time for growth and a time for rest; a time of flourishing and a time of waiting to flourish. Creation reminds us how little we are and how big God is. Jesus tells us to consider the birds, and see the way that God cares for the needs of some of the smallest around us. So, too, will God take care of our needs (Matthew 6:26-34).

As parents and spiritual guides for the little people in our lives, it is our responsibility to share the testimony of creation as the psalmist does. We have this wonderful and unique opportunity to watch as our children experience the world around them for the first time, and every time they respond in awe, may we remember just how amazing the world is at capturing the wonder and magnificence of the Creator.

Blessing

May God's creation bring you great joy as you stand in awe of all there is to see. May the beauty, order, and magnitude of the world teach you about God, and may it always remind you that the God of the universe cares for you.

Reflection

Keep an eye out for the ways that God wants to encourage you through creation today.

Psalm 20

6 Now I know that the Lord will help his anointed;
he will answer him from his holy heaven
with mighty victories by his right hand.

7 Some take pride in chariots, and some in horses,
but our pride is in the name of the Lord our God.

8 They will collapse and fall,
but we shall rise and stand upright.

9 Give victory to the king, O Lord;
answer us when we call.

Truth

This psalm opens with a blessing, a prayer that the faithful would be blessed by God, their prayers for help answered, and their plans fulfilled, not unlike the blessings included so far in this book. If you have some extra time, the blessing in verse 1-5 is quite beautiful. In fact, the whole psalm is rich with the promises of God, and David's steadfast faith and hope shine throughout. I can't help but think of David's circumstances every time I read one of his psalms. This was a man chosen by God. He was unassuming, forgotten by his own family, and God chose him to be king over Israel. Yet despite this grand anointing, David spent much of his time before becoming king running for his life. Can you imagine that? If he is supposed to be king one day, why is he hiding in caves and fearing for his life?

David laments over this very thing in many of his psalms, but his faith remains steadfast. He knows the Lord will help the anointed. David knows better than most the mighty power of God. He sees God as a fierce warrior, fighting the battles of the faithful and protecting them from enemies. Unlike the warriors David faces on the battlefield, he doesn't put his trust in his own strength or weaponry, he trusts in the strength of God to deliver him. In some of his darkest days, David remains confident that God will give the victory to the anointed, to those who are faithful.

While we may not be running for our lives as David was, we face challenges and interpersonal interactions every day that weigh on us. In times of hardship, frustration, and despair, it's important to remember who we are: the beloved and anointed children of God.

Blessing

May you trust always in the strength of your Creator. May you not exalt earthly idols of power, but instead trust the steadfast love and might of God alone. May you call out to God in your troubles, may you hold strong to hope and experience God's deliverance.

Reflection

How often do you put your faith in earthly systems that promise safety and security? Is this something you elevate over the power of God in your life?

Psalm 21

---

1 In your strength the king rejoices, O Lord,
  and in your help how greatly he exults!

2 You have given him his heart's desire,
  and have not withheld the request of his lips.

3 For you meet him with rich blessings;
  you set a crown of fine gold on his head.

4 He asked you for life; you gave it to him—
  length of days forever and ever.

5 His glory is great through your help;
  splendor and majesty you bestow on him.

6 You bestow on him blessings forever;
  you make him glad with the joy of your presence.

7 For the king trusts in the Lord,
  and through the steadfast love of the Most High he shall not be moved.

Truth

Unlike some of the other psalms that we have encountered together, in Psalm 21 we find the king humbly responding to what God has done, fully recognizing that it is God who provided the success and victory that he has won. At this moment, the king's spiritual health is at a high point. Since we all want to be spiritually healthy, let's look at the elements of the king's description and talk about applying them in our own life. The overarching themes are dependence and gratitude.

Verse 1 mentions God's strength and help; verse 7, the king's trust in the Lord; and verse 4 the king's confidence to ask for what he wanted, and God responding by giving it to him. Each one of these verses is an example of his dependence on God. Spiritually healthy people receive their strength from God, trust that the Lord is working in their lives, and courageously ask knowing that God is the ultimate provider. As we move towards spiritual health we must leave our independence behind and seek Christ.

Even so, dependence on God is only a piece of spiritual health. Another is how we respond to what God is doing in our lives. The king responds here with joy and gratitude. I have found practicing gratitude is an amazing way to find hope and contentment in the ups and downs of life. When I can look around at what God has provided for me and be thankful, my superfluous desires fade away. Finally, when we spend significant time with someone or something that is life-giving, the presence of that thing gives joy. Like the psalmist, I hope our time in God's presence is characterized by joy.

Blessing

May you learn to depend on the Lord early in your life. May you confidently trust God with all of your heart and may that trust lead to a peace that surpasses all understanding. May you notice the work that the Lord is doing in your life and may you respond with gratitude and joy.

Reflection

Do you feel spiritually healthy in this season? In what ways can you seek spiritual health in this season?

Psalm 22

9 Yet it was you who took me from the womb;
you kept me safe on my mother's breast.

10 On you I was cast from my birth,
and since my mother bore me you have been my God.

11 Do not be far from me,
for trouble is near
and there is no one to help...

29 To him, indeed, shall all who sleep in the earth bow down;
before him shall bow all who go down to the dust,
and I shall live for him.

30 Posterity will serve him;
future generations will be told about the Lord,

31 and proclaim his deliverance to a people yet unborn,
saying that he has done it.

Truth

David opens this psalm with the heart-wrenching lament, "My God, my God, why have you forsaken me?" David feels utterly alone. His enemies are surrounding him, and he is mocked and cast low. It is this psalm that Jesus is quoting when he cries out to God on the cross (Matthew 27:26, Mark 15:34). When we read this psalm, we can imagine utter despair, a feeling of being completely forsaken by God. But what David knows is that even when we feel abandoned, God has not actually left us alone. Because of this faith, David is able to continue to plead with God to draw near to him, to comfort him, and to defeat his enemies.

Despite feeling hopeless, David knows that God has anointed him, and intimately known him and the path of his life since before he was born. David closes the psalm with praise, saying that one day all will bow down before the one true God. David pledges to live his life for God, despite his circumstances. And he speaks boldly of the legacy of God's people: that future generations, children yet to be born, will speak of all that God has done and will praise the Creator.

When we observe the pain of the psalmist and remember Jesus quoting this psalm on the cross, we are reminded both of the pain that comes as part of life, and the hope that we have in a God who came and journeyed alongside. God is a God of deliverance and still journeys alongside us through the presence of the Holy Spirit.

Blessing

May you remember the mighty works of God. May you draw near to your Creator in times of loneliness and despair. May you praise God and proclaim the promises of deliverance despite your circumstances, holding fast to hope and faith above all things.

Reflection

Have you felt this same kind of utter despair that David speaks about in this psalm? What do you do when you feel as if God has left you abandoned?

May They Be Blessed

Psalm 23

1 The Lord is my shepherd, I shall not want.

2 He makes me lie down in green pastures;
  he leads me beside still waters;

3 he restores my soul.
  He leads me in right paths
  for his name's sake.

Truth

Psalm 23 may be one of the most well-known psalms and for good reason. For the psalmist, it represents moments of pure tranquility. With an artistic metaphor, the psalmist describes the way in which the Lord cares for him, which in turn describes the way that God cares for us.

In the first three verses, the psalmist describes five ways that God cares for us. When we put God first in our life, verse 1 says our other desires are fleeting. They pale in comparison to what God has for us. Verse 2 says that the shepherd "makes" us lie down. In Hebrew, the sense here is not so much that God forces us to rest, but rather that because of the way God cares for us we are able to rest. Rest isn't only God's desire for us but also is intricately tied to creation. Remember that on the 7th day God rested (Gen 2:2-3). If the Creator of the world values rest, shouldn't we? In the second part of verse 2, we see that God cares for us by leading us to still waters. As we touched upon in Psalm 1, water is used as a symbol in the psalms of the life that we receive from God our source.

Time spent with Jesus (verse 3) restores our soul. In fact, while things in life can bring us joy, true restoration comes from resting in the Lord. Lastly, we rest in the final promise of verse 3, that the Lord will guide us through our life if we are willing to follow. Sometimes the path is foggy and unclear, but we will be led down the right path when we follow the Shepherd.

Overall, Psalm 23 is a reminder of how important it is to stay close to the shepherd. When we journey closely with Jesus, we can go forth in peace knowing that we will be cared for.

Blessing

May you always stay close to Jesus your shepherd. May you know peace, goodness, rest, and restoration while you journey. And, when the trail is foggy and you aren't sure what's next, may you find hope in the truth that you are walking in the steps of the One who loves you enough to give up everything on your behalf.

Reflection

Are you tired and weary? Do you need to rest? May the Lord in this season restore your soul.

Psalm 24

*1 The earth is the Lord's and all that is in it,
  the world, and those who live in it;*

*2 for he has founded it on the seas,
  and established it on the rivers.*

*3 Who shall ascend the hill of the Lord?
  And who shall stand in his holy place?*

*4 Those who have clean hands and pure hearts,
  who do not lift up their souls to what is false,
  and do not swear deceitfully.*

*5 They will receive blessing from the Lord,
  and vindication from the God of their salvation.*

Truth

Scripture is filled with descriptions of God's transcendence: God is above us, seated on a high throne, a holy mountain, a ruler of the heavenly realm. And though I know these words well, I don't often sit in them, reflecting on the holiness of God. Do I live my life as if everything around me, all that I am and all that I have, belongs to God? Do I act as if God controls the elements and created everything that has life on earth? Of course, I know it. I've read these words in scripture for most of my life, but do I let the profundity of that truth seep into my actions? Because when I stop, really stop, and let the vastness of God sink in, what other response is there than the one David gives us here? To shout praises, to proclaim God as the King of glory, to stand in awe of all that God encompasses.

And to think, we, as believers, are invited to ascend God's holy mountain, to enter the temple. It's astounding. And that same God purifies our hearts and hands so that we might one day see God face to face. As humans, it is a daily struggle to not lift our hearts to false things. The world promises quick fixes and an illusion of safety, but God promises so much more. God promises salvation and blessing and communion with the One who holds all of eternity.

Blessing

May you know the great depths of God's love for you. May you stand in awe of the created world and all that has been set in motion by our holy and good God. May you lift your heart to the One who is the ultimate provider, refuge, and King.

Reflection

Have you taken the time lately to reflect on the greatness of God? How does this shift in perspective change the way you approach your relationship with God?

Psalm 25

4 Make me to know your ways, O Lord;
teach me your paths.

5 Lead me in your truth, and teach me,
for you are the God of my salvation;
for you I wait all day long.

12 Who are they that fear the Lord?
He will teach them the way that they should choose.

13 They will abide in prosperity,
and their children shall possess the land.

14 The friendship of the Lord is for those who fear him,
and he makes his covenant known to them.

Truth

Fear is a common yet complicated term used throughout the Bible. Most of the time when the Bible uses the word "fear" in reference to God, it means the way that humans relate and respond to God's greatness. Without diving too deeply into the original Hebrew, but giving a fuller sense of what the psalmist is getting at when using the term, fear is deeply tied to worship. So instead of terror and dread, Biblical fear is more like reverence, awe, and complete and absolute allegiance to God. When the Bible speaks of fearing God, it usually means being captivated by God, who is by very nature an unfathomable and infinite creative power, the source of everything that is known and unknown.

And the craziest part about it is that this God of measureless power and knowledge desires to be in an intimate relationship with you. In response to this, the psalmist asks God to help him understand that which God has for him. The psalmist is so arrested and enthralled by God that he seeks God every moment of the day, watching where God might be leading, and asking God to continue to point out the ways that he as a follower and friend of God can grow.

We are encouraged, knowing we too have been covenanted to God. God promises that when we draw near in "fear," we will flourish. When we seek God's way, it will be shown. And when our children see the way that God captures our hearts and brings delight to our lives, they too will know the love of God.

Blessing

May you be captivated by the glory of God and may the depth of God's love take root in your life. May you always seek God's path for your life and as you progress in your faith, may you know that you have a friend in your Lord and Savior Jesus Christ.

Reflection

How does it make you feel to know that Jesus Christ calls you friend?

Psalm 26

*1 Vindicate me, O Lord,
for I have walked in my integrity,
and I have trusted in the Lord without wavering.*

*2 Prove me, O Lord, and try me;
test my heart and mind.*

*3 For your steadfast love is before my eyes,
and I walk in faithfulness to you.*

*4 I do not sit with the worthless,
nor do I consort with hypocrites;*

*5 I hate the company of evildoers,
and will not sit with the wicked.*

*6 I wash my hands in innocence,
and go around your altar, O Lord,*

*7 singing aloud a song of thanksgiving,
and telling all your wondrous deeds.*

Truth

This psalm has an interesting tone. David is pleading with God to show him the justice he deserves, to save him as a righteous man amidst sinners. Now, at first, to our modern ways of thinking, this passage can almost sound arrogant. David is talking about how much more righteous he is than others and how he has resisted falling to the ways of the world in order to be faithful to God. As modern Christians, we're entrenched with the rhetoric of humans being sinners. Christ came to save us while we were still sinners, and we are unworthy of being saved, so great is the love of Christ.

So this passage can be confusing to hold and learn from in light of what we hear in church.

But when we read the psalms, it's important to not only consider context, but also the purpose and the literary style of the writing. The psalms are poetry, and to take them at literal face value is to miss the underlying point of them. I don't believe that David is saying here that he is better than everyone around him, so God should save him. I believe David is using hyperbolic language to describe how alone he feels. He sees wickedness in the world, and in his attempt to be righteous, he feels like he is alone, the only righteous one left. Likewise, David is on a journey to understand the mysterious ways of God. He has cried out to God to bring wrath upon his enemies, to fight his battles, and David has seen the mighty strength of God. But he has also seen evil prevail and good people perish. God's ways don't often make sense to us, and in this psalm, David is not a man who is assured of his deliverance despite his acts of faithfulness. I think what we see in this psalm is a journey of David's faith and understanding, and even his hopeful declaration that he will continue to be the person of faith he is, despite his circumstances.

Blessing
May you rest always in the salvation of Jesus Christ. May you be in awe of the mysterious ways of God while knowing that Christ has already paid the price for you. May you draw near to God in times of loneliness and be ever curious in your desire to know God more deeply.

Reflection
Have you ever felt lonely in your walk with God? Has it ever felt like God lets evil go unnoticed in the world?

Psalm 27

1 The Lord is my light and my salvation;
* whom shall I fear?*
The Lord is the stronghold of my life;
* of whom shall I be afraid?*

9 Do not hide your face from me.
* Do not turn your servant away in anger,*
* you who have been my help.*
* Do not cast me off, do not forsake me,*
* O God of my salvation!*

13 I believe that I shall see the goodness of the Lord
* in the land of the living.*

14 Wait for the Lord;
* be strong, and let your heart take courage;*
* wait for the Lord!*

Truth

Often when we think of the psalmist, we think of a very confident and faithful person, but it's important to remember that, like us, the psalmist is on a journey as well. The psalmist expresses fearful anxiety as he weighs potential outcomes and seeks God's protection. Even though in verse 3 the psalmist claims to not be fearful, this seems to be more of a hope than a present reality. The key takeaway for us lies in verse 13, which says that when we pursue Christ, we can have what God intends for us even now. Eternal salvation and relationship with God will be incredible, but the promise is that we get to experience and multiply the goodness of God in this world, "in the land of the living," right now.

    This is one of the great and beautiful things about being spiritual leaders in our homes. With our kids, we have the opportunity to both witness to them through the ups and downs of our journey and invite them along for the ride. Due to the way children interact and interpret the world around them, the things they observe set a precedent for them of the way life is and should be. If they are only allowed to see the good and easy parts of our Christian journey, they will experience extreme tension when their own journey is not easy. Parents may think that sharing doubt about their faith with their kids is like puncturing the hull of a ship; it will sink a child's faith. However, the opposite is actually true. Parents can help normalize doubt for their children by allowing them to watch how they work through it. This brings us full circle to Psalm 27. The psalmist experiences and struggles with doubt, yet what matters is his response of belief and of seeking God's shelter, even in the middle of doubt, because God will see us through the storm. Don't worry about poking holes in your children's faith, instead teach ways to reinforce it.

Blessing

My prayer is that you will witness my journey with Jesus and that I will find the courage to invite you into even the most vulnerable parts. May you grow quicker and greater in your faith and may you too share your journey with those around you one day. I pray that even now you would know the goodness of God and as you grow older you would find eternal joy and security in each present moment.

Reflection

Have you thought about how you will intentionally share your spiritual journey with your kids?

Psalm 28

6 Blessed be the Lord,
  for he has heard the sound of my pleadings.

7 The Lord is my strength and my shield;
  in him my heart trusts;
  so I am helped, and my heart exults,
  and with my song I give thanks to him.

8 The Lord is the strength of his people;
  he is the saving refuge of his anointed.

9 O save your people, and bless your heritage;
  be their shepherd, and carry them forever.

Truth

The psalm begins with David pleading for God to hear his cries and to repay the sinful people he sees in the world justly. It's fascinating to read the psalms of David and watch so many of his most human emotions play out in the text. Though David was writing rich Hebrew poetry, he did not shy away from his raw emotions. We still are seeing him work through the complicated ways of God. But then in verse 6, David pivots. Despite his frustration, despite his lack of understanding, he praises the name of God.

Even while David is still in the midst of hardship, he declares that God has still heard him. He is holding onto faith based on the fact that he has already seen God at work. He has seen God deliver the faithful and fight for the vulnerable, and he knows God will do it again. David, a warrior in his own right, doesn't rely on his own strength or weaponry. Because of what he's seen and because of what he knows to be true of God, his heart trusts in the strength of God. Throughout the Old Testament, we see the heroes of the faith, like Moses, Joshua, Samuel, and the prophets, tell the people to remember. Remember what God has done for you, remember your deliverance, because it's only through remembering what God has already done that we can stay faithful in times of hardship. Despite the opening of this psalm, David is choosing to praise God as he remembers what God has already done. God is the same yesterday, today, and tomorrow. What God has done for the anointed, God will do again.

Blessing

May you trust always in the strength of God. May you remember the great works that God does in your life, and remember God's steadfastness in times of trouble. May you praise the name of God, who delivers you and saves you and fights for you.

Reflection

Do you take the time to remember what God has done in your life? Do these acts of remembrance serve to strengthen your faith in times of darkness?

Psalm 29

2 Ascribe to the Lord the glory of his name;
  worship the Lord in holy splendor.

3 The voice of the Lord is over the waters;
  the God of glory thunders,
  the Lord, over mighty waters.

4 The voice of the Lord is powerful;
  the voice of the Lord is full of majesty.

10 The Lord sits enthroned over the flood;
  the Lord sits enthroned as king forever.

11 May the Lord give strength to his people!
  May the Lord bless his people with peace!

Truth

"In the beginning when God created the heavens and the earth, the earth was a formless void and darkness covered the face of the deep, while a wind from God swept over the face of the waters. Then God said…" (Genesis 1:1-3)

Psalm 29 thunders with God's unfathomable power. God's power to speak and in so doing create. God's power to speak and in so doing destroy. The power to speak and in so doing change a life. The power to speak and to have those who barely know Him lay down their nets and follow. Sometimes it's hard to remember that God is powerful. In fact, many in our culture look around at the ugliness and brokenness of the world and conclude that God is impotent rather than omnipotent. Usually, this is because it is so hard for us as humans to experience the horrors and atrocities that sinful, broken people bring into this world and reconcile that with an all-loving God. And yet, by pulling in creation language, the psalmist reminds us that God created the world intentionally and that God's power is on display in every part of creation.

In the Christian faith, we celebrate that God created the world with divine relationship in mind. Yet, while God created us specifically for relationship, in all of God's power, God gave us choice, and humanity chose self-interest and separation, and so the sinful slippery slope began. So, the psalmist is reminding us of both the reason for which we were created and the power that's on display in the way in which we were created. Second, the psalmist reminds us that God's power can be seen in nature all around us– in the crashing waves, in the blizzards, in the wind, and in the thunder. How much more powerful must be their Creator? Be encouraged and know that this all-mighty, selfless being is completely for you.

Blessing

May you choose intimacy. May you choose relationship. May you choose to receive and reciprocate the love of God. God created you in God's image, God gave you the power of choice, and God desires to be in relationship with you so desperately that God did everything in God's power to reconcile that which sin separates.

Reflection

Where do you see God's power at work? Where do you need God's power to show up in your life?

Psalm 30

*4 Sing praises to the Lord, O you his faithful ones,
and give thanks to his holy name.*

*5 For his anger is but for a moment;
his favor is for a lifetime.
Weeping may linger for the night,
but joy comes with the morning.*

*11 You have turned my mourning into dancing;
you have taken off my sackcloth
and clothed me with joy,*

*12 so that my soul may praise you and not be silent.
O Lord my God, I will give thanks to you forever.*

Truth

The choruses of praise and thanksgiving found in this psalm always stir something in me. Maybe it's the resonance of the refrains we still sing in church today or the bold declaration of faith, but when I read these words from David, I feel connected to the ancient church and people of God. Despite how removed modern Christians are today from the Hebrew people or the first followers of Jesus, there is common ground and connectedness through the work of the Spirit and the truth of who God is.

We, as people of God, can join the chorus of praise, declaring that God's love and salvation bring new joy for us. God's favor is upon the faithful and that means our joy comes from a source much deeper than circumstance. And when we do face despair, we still have hope. We still have a God who can take our mourning and our pain and draw purpose from it, placing it in the context of a grander plan that our human minds can't yet comprehend. God turns our mourning into dancing. David has seen it, and those who know God have seen it in their lives. What other response is there but to praise God and give thanks for all that God has done?

Be encouraged today by the truth that God is the source of our joy and, when we are tired, frustrated, or burdened, we can lean into the timeless community of God that has, is, and will always give thanks for all that God is doing. When we are weak, may we lean in because the promise is that joy comes in the morning.

Blessing

May you praise the name of God, holding fast to hope in God's unchanging ways and the legacy of faith. May you know that part of your inheritance is participating in the timeless community of God.

Reflection

Take a moment to think about the grand community of saints that you are a part of because of your identity in Christ. When was the last time you leaned in to your church community in a time of need or extended a helping hand to someone who was in need of joy?

Psalm 31

19 O how abundant is your goodness
 that you have laid up for those who fear you,
 and accomplished for those who take refuge in you,
 in the sight of everyone!

21 Blessed be the Lord,
 for he has wondrously shown his steadfast love to me
 when I was beset as a city under siege.

Truth

How abundant is God's goodness? Even though it should come as no surprise, I am always so amazed by the way that the Holy Spirit speaks through scripture. I began working through this Psalm over two weeks ago and the difference between the two ways that I received holy encouragement then and now is staggering. I am reminded that we each come to the word of God with different postures and from different places and yet the Holy Spirit always has something for us. The fact that the Holy Spirit is with us, knows what we need, and speaks to us through God's word is part of God's abundant goodness.

Sometimes when we come to the text we are empty. This is where I was two weeks ago. I needed God to be my refuge. I just wanted to curl up in the loving arms of God and leave all my worries, responsibilities, and struggles at the door. The pressures around me weighed heavily on my soul. I felt like a city under siege. At that moment, God's abundant goodness was only a future promise, not a present reality. A glimmer of hope that while I may not feel it now, at the core of God is goodness. It's in these times we are met with God's presence.

Sometimes, when we come to the text, we are full. We have

experienced love and joy, which are gifts from the Creator. We may be in awe and fear of all that God has done and feeling blessed. This is where I am today, reminded that Jesus is steadfast in the way that He walks with us as we journey and that He is a beacon of God's goodness that gets us through the hard times.

Be encouraged by the truth that God's abundant goodness is a past, present, and future reality. Whether you are full or empty today, God is present with you.

Blessing

May you know God's abundant love. When you are empty, may you feel the embrace of your Creator, and when you are full may you go forth sharing the love and joy that you have with those around you. May you be like Jesus, a steadfast friend, a beacon of hope for others, and when you don't feel it for yourself, may you seek the light of Christ that never fades.

Reflection

Today, are you empty, full, or somewhere in between? Ask the Holy Spirit to meet you where you are right now.

Psalm 32

1 Happy are those whose transgression is forgiven,
   whose sin is covered.

2 Happy are those to whom the Lord imputes no iniquity,
   and in whose spirit there is no deceit.

3 While I kept silence, my body wasted away
   through my groaning all day long.

4 For day and night your hand was heavy upon me;
   my strength was dried up as by the heat of summer. Selah

5 Then I acknowledged my sin to you,
   and I did not hide my iniquity;

I said, "I will confess my transgressions to the Lord,"
   and you forgave the guilt of my sin...

10 Many are the torments of the wicked,
   but steadfast love surrounds those who trust in the Lord.

11 Be glad in the Lord and rejoice, O righteous,
   and shout for joy, all you upright in heart.

Truth

I find confession to be an uncomfortable part of the Christian life, and I'd venture that I'm not alone in this feeling. There is so much freedom in the forgiveness given to us by Jesus and in the grace and mercy of God. Daily I can look to the scriptures and be humbled by my humanity, acknowledging my sin and shortcomings and realizing that I am made whole only through the grace of God and the work of Christ. It's a truth that compels me to praise God in the same way that David does in the closing of this psalm. But the reality of true, biblical confession, coming before God and, at times, brothers and sisters in Christ, to confess and clearly lay out the mistakes and sins I've committed, that's not as joyful. Doesn't God know everything about me anyway? Do I really need to confess the details of my sin? Can't I just ask for forgiveness and move on? I'll admit there are times when I've done this, but though God's forgiveness is more broad and all-encompassing than I can fathom, it is confession and acknowledgment of where I missed the mark that leads to repentance. And it's in repentance where we find godly freedom.

David puts it so beautifully here. Keeping silent does us no favors; our spirit wastes away while the weight of our sin entraps us. That is not God's intention for us, and it becomes clear in the freedom we experience through godly confession. We are not meant to be tormented, we can be glad in the Lord, free to rejoice and repent and live the life we were created to live.

Blessing

May you be bold and vulnerable and honest before God, trusting in God's ability to forgive you and make you new. May you practice and know the freedom of repentance and the joy of forgiveness. And may you extend forgiveness to all of God's people as you grow into a person of humility, grace, and mercy.

Reflection

Do you practice confession and repentance with God? Have you ever felt weighed down by sin? Do you know God is waiting to forgive you?

Psalm 33

4 For the word of the Lord is upright,
  and all his work is done in faithfulness.

5 He loves righteousness and justice;
  the earth is full of the steadfast love of the Lord.

Truth

Verse 4 is about God's character and the psalmist wants to convey the goodness that animates God's actions. By saying that the word of the Lord is upright, the psalmist means that God speaks, and goodness flows forth. In noting that everything God does is done faithfully, the psalmist means that God is consistent. In everything that God has done, is doing, and will do, God is steady, unchanging, and dependable. This may seem like a bit of a funny thing to point out about God, but I resonate deeply with it because it is sometimes hard to remember that God's character is always the same. When someone dies from starvation, God is still provider. When an innocent person is shot down in the street, God is still just. When people do unspeakable things in the name of Jesus, God is still righteous. When we experience the hate of another, God is still love. And when things seem to be falling apart and we don't know where to turn, God is still hope.

Psalm 33 reminds us that in spite of our broken world, God never changes. God is the lover of your soul; Jesus is the wounded healer of the world. The God of the Old Testament is the same God that we see in Jesus, you were created by the same God that sent Jesus to die on the cross for your sins. Not only is God's character unchanging, but all of creation is infused with God's essence. This concept can seem obscure, but if you take a moment to think about your child, it is hard to deny that God is still doing great things in the world. The world can be a hard and challenging place, but God is still good. As Revelation 21:5 says, God is faithful and is making all things new.

Blessing

May you know that the God who gave you to me is good. May you know that God never changes. God desperately loved you yesterday, deeply loves you today, and will lovingly pursue you for the rest of your life. As the world bends and twists around you, know that God is stable and can be trusted to always be working towards reconciling the world back into relationship with God.

Reflection

Name one or two unchanging characteristics of God for which you are thankful.

Psalm 34

11 Come, O children, listen to me;
  I will teach you the fear of the Lord.

12 Which of you desires life,
  and covets many days to enjoy good?

13 Keep your tongue from evil,
  and your lips from speaking deceit.

14 Depart from evil, and do good;
  seek peace, and pursue it.

15 The eyes of the Lord are on the righteous,
  and his ears are open to their cry.

16 The face of the Lord is against evildoers,
  to cut off the remembrance of them from the earth.

17 When the righteous cry for help, the Lord hears,
  and rescues them from all their troubles.

18 The Lord is near to the brokenhearted,
  and saves the crushed in spirit.

Truth

There's so much about parenting that feels like guesswork. You can ask for advice, read dozens of books, but at the end of the day, when it's just you and this small impressionable human that God has entrusted to you, it can be agonizing as you try to discern what is best. There are so many methods, so much contradictory advice out there, and it's overwhelming. As parents, we know we are not perfect, and despite our fierce love for our children and the best of intentions, there are going to be areas where we fall short and don't make the right call. And it's for this very reason that parenting with a reliance on God and ultimately entrusting your child to God is a much better method than whatever advice a book or parenting blog can give you. Those are valuable resources, but the truth is that scripture gives us the fundamental building blocks for how to raise our children and what we should instill in the next generation of Christ-followers.

You can forget to sign your kids up for swim lessons, feed them non-organic food, and give them too much screen time, but you will do right by your children if you teach them to fear the Lord, to depart from what is evil and cling to what is good, to seek peace and pursue it. As a parent, I try to meditate on these words. Am I teaching my children to seek peace? Am I teaching them to fear God, and am I doing it in both deed and word? This is where our focus should be as we keep our eyes on Jesus.

Blessing

May you fear the Lord and know deeply the love that God has for you. May you strive for goodness and peace in your life, showing grace and mercy to all people who reflect the very nature and image of God. May you put your faith always in the God who hears your calls and will rescue you in times of trouble.

Reflection

Do you find yourself getting caught up in the demands and choices of modern parenting? Are you able to focus instead on how to instill a love of God in your children?

Psalm 35

11 Malicious witnesses rise up;
  they ask me about things I do not know.

12 They repay me evil for good;
  my soul is forlorn.

13 But as for me, when they were sick,
  I wore sackcloth;
  I afflicted myself with fasting.
  I prayed with head bowed on my bosom,

14 as though I grieved for a friend or a brother;
  I went about as one who laments for a mother,
  bowed down and in mourning.

17 How long, O Lord, will you look on?

Truth

As we have seen, the Book of Psalms is filled with all kinds of prayers and proclamations to God. The two most prevalent are praise (prayers of gratitude and worship) and lament. Lament is a word that is often misunderstood and/or left out of Christian worship in our contemporary context, mostly because true lament can be uncomfortable and countercultural. In a culture that prizes strength, confidence, self-assurance, emotional stoicism (especially for boys), and independence, lament is to be avoided like the plague. But all throughout the Bible God encourages and participates in lamenting the things in this world that aren't as God created them to be.

To lament is to grieve with God and with others. Daniel Hill writes, "To lament is to acknowledge the pain that we aren't home and that this world is too often marked by evil and injustice. To lament is to ask God the haunting questions "'Where are you? What are you doing? How long must we wait?'"* We are encouraged to lament over what is not right in the world and grieve with those around us. Interestingly the psalmist both laments to God about the way he has been treated and describes the way he lamented with and for those who betrayed him. This is a powerful and convicting picture because the psalmist laments with the very people who betray him. You could say he comes alongside his enemies, he showed up, bared his heart, and grieved with those who probably would not have done the same for him. The conviction lies in the truth that the church rarely laments with those that they hold close, not to mention those they consider to be their enemies.

In verse 17, the psalmist asks, "How long, O Lord, will you look on?" This haunting question acknowledges that things aren't consistent with our understanding of who God is, and it's this dissonance that we grieve. The topic of lament and grief may not be the encouragement you came looking for today. But, in grieving with one another, we step closer to who God created us to be and into the community that is the body of Christ. May the heavy-laden share their yoke and may those whose yokes are light help carry it.

Blessing

May you not be afraid to lament and grieve the things in this world that don't line up with the way God intended them to be. May you be comforted by our Savior who wept, and who encourages us to follow His example. May you step boldly into your emotions and may God use your tears to change the world.

Reflection

How comfortable are you grieving with others? Ask God to continue to transform your heart to be like Christ's.

*Hill, Daniel. White Awake: An Honest Look at What It Means to Be White (pp. 114-115). InterVarsity Press. Kindle Edition.

Psalm 36

1 Transgression speaks to the wicked
  deep in their hearts;
 there is no fear of God
  before their eyes.

2 For they flatter themselves in their own eyes
 that their iniquity cannot be found out and hated.

3 The words of their mouths are mischief and deceit;
 they have ceased to act wisely and do good.

4 They plot mischief while on their beds;
 they are set on a way that is not good;
 they do not reject evil.

5 Your steadfast love, O Lord, extends to the heavens,
 your faithfulness to the clouds.

6 Your righteousness is like the mighty mountains,
 your judgments are like the great deep;
 you save humans and animals alike, O Lord.

Truth

Unfortunately, we see evil in our world every day. The internet and the 24-hour news cycle has made it inescapable. The evil we see also exists in us. Despite God's plan for humanity, because of our sin, we have fallen short. In fact, Paul tells us that all have sinned and fallen short of the glory of God (Romans 3:23). But in contrast to our human sinfulness, God is faithful. God is faithful to the point of forgiveness and deliverance and unconditional love, and the most faithful act of all: God sent Jesus to redeem humanity.

Though the God of the Bible carries down judgment for those

who are unrepentant of their wickedness and unaccepting of Jesus's redemptive work, God's ultimate goal is to restore creation and God's relationship with all of creation. The psalmist says God saves humans and animals alike and is redeeming all things. It's difficult to imagine, but as the psalmist describes in the rest of the passage, all people may take refuge in God. The most wicked among us can repent and move forward into right relationship with God, and they will find salvation and healing and abundant life. This is at times a frustrating truth to grapple with, as our human minds want to rank some sin worse than others, some people worse than others. But as so much of the Bible makes clear, none of us is worthy of the steadfast love of God, and yet we are all able to receive it.

Blessing

May you encounter the fierce and unchanging love of God in tangible ways. May you be humbled by your humanness and cling to God because God loves you and will always be a refuge for you. May you receive the forgiveness of God and be eager to share that forgiveness with others, because all people are made in God's image.

Reflection

Take a minute to think about a time when you were incorrectly judged by another. Forgive them. Take a minute to think about a time you inappropriately judged someone. Ask for God's forgiveness and receive the freedom found in God's steadfast love for you.

Psalm 37

1 Do not fret because of the wicked;
do not be envious of wrongdoers,

2 for they will soon fade like the grass,
and wither like the green herb.

3 Trust in the Lord, and do good;
so you will live in the land, and enjoy security.

4 Take delight in the Lord,
and he will give you the desires of your heart.

Truth

I don't know about you, but I am definitely guilty of envy from time to time, especially when it comes to those whose lives are steeped in extreme success and wealth. While being successful and wealthy by no means equates to wickedness, it seems like those who shine brightest in our culture's limelight do indeed fade over time. Yet, the focus of this Psalm isn't to critique those we perceive as wicked or wrongdoers, but rather to challenge us to examine our own hearts to uncover the reasons that we envy or wish for a different life. If we unpack verses 3 and 4, we can reverse engineer three reasons that we may find ourselves wistful or envious.

Verse 3 encourages us to trust the Lord and do good. When we see and are envious of the success of other people, it is often because we have a hard time trusting that the life God has for us will be similarly as great. Also, we may compare the other person's actions and morals against our own, concluding that it isn't fair that they have more or have it better when we have worked as hard or harder. This boils down to self-righteousness, selfishness, and a lack of faith in what God is doing in our own lives. The correction in this psalm is that we learn to act not for ourselves but for others, and trust God, believing that God has a plan and knows what's best.

Ultimately, when we really examine our hearts, all of this is often associated with what it is we delight in. In other words, the place where we go for happiness tends to be the source of our goals and aspirations. When we succumb to the materialistic and consumeristic ideals of our culture, we are distracted from the One from whom we should be seeking delight. We are promised that as our hearts shift to look more like the heart of Christ, our desires will move toward intimacy instead of isolation, toward helping others instead of comparing ourselves with others, and toward a life whose wealth is measured by love instead of things. To this end, God will enrich our lives and the desires of our heart will be met.

Blessing

May your heart be set on higher things than that which our culture promotes. May your desires align with the heart of Christ. May you seek intimacy over isolation; kindness and care over selfishness; and may your life be rich with God's love.

Reflection

Have you ever found yourself envious of another? How can shifting your source of delight help you to refocus the desires of your heart?

Psalm 38

9 *O Lord, all my longing is known to you;*
   my sighing is not hidden from you.

10 *My heart throbs, my strength fails me;*
   as for the light of my eyes—it also has gone from me.

11 *My friends and companions stand aloof from my affliction,*
   and my neighbors stand far off...

17 *For I am ready to fall,*
   and my pain is ever with me.

18 *I confess my iniquity;*
   I am sorry for my sin.

19 *Those who are my foes without cause are mighty,*
   and many are those who hate me wrongfully.

20 *Those who render me evil for good*
   are my adversaries because I follow after good.

21 *Do not forsake me, O Lord;*
   O my God, do not be far from me;

22 *make haste to help me,*
   O Lord, my salvation.

Truth

David does not hide his anguish in this psalm. He uses figurative, and frankly a bit graphic, language to illustrate his misery. He speaks of festering wounds, burning loins, ears that do not hear, and an inability to speak. He cries out, he feels that everyone, his neighbors and allies, has turned their backs on him as his enemies grow stronger. Despite the crushing loneliness and wasting despair that David feels, he trusts in God, who knows all of his longings. That phrase stopped me in my tracks when I first read through it. David laments with God throughout the entire book of psalms, but it struck me that even with how much David has cried out to God in prayer, there is still misery and heartbreak left unsaid, things too painful to utter, hope too outlandish to speak out loud. Not only does God hear us, our audible cries in the darkest night, God also knows our longings, our groanings too deep for words.

David is without any strength left to fight. He has been so bruised by the battle and faced so much defeat that he can do nothing more than sigh in silence in God's presence. We don't see David turn to praise and thanksgiving in this psalm. He pleads with God to not repay his sin with wrath. He asks for mercy, for a quick delivery from his pain. And we, as readers, are left to sit in David's lament, stewing in his loneliness, without words to comfort or praise to speak. It's an uncomfortable place to be, but I'm grateful for the reminders and the example to lay ourselves bare before God. It's the only way towards true repentance and intimacy with God.

Blessing

May you know the comfort of God. May you come before God with your praise and with your lament, trusting in God to meet you in the midst of your darkest emotions. And may you fix your eyes always on God, trusting in the steadfast love that has been true through the ages.

Reflection

Can you empathize with David's deep despair in this psalm? Do you come before God raw in your honesty and unable to speak, trusting in God to comfort you and deliver you?

Psalm 39

4 "Lord, let me know my end,
  and what is the measure of my days;
  let me know how fleeting my life is.

5 You have made my days a few handbreadths,
  and my lifetime is as nothing in your sight.
  Surely everyone stands as a mere breath.

7 "And now, O Lord, what do I wait for?
  My hope is in you.

Truth

On first blush these verses from Psalm 39 feel quite odd, rather morbid, yet whimsical. In American culture, we are happy to celebrate a new life but are quite uncomfortable with death. There is something about the end of life that haunts some part of our present. Its influence is at times barely discernible, but there are times when our anxiety over the grave hovers nearby. The wisdom literature and culture of the Old Testament is much better at discussing death than we are in our contemporary context. This psalm invites us to ponder these things because, when we hold our mortality in tension with the reality of who God is, we can discard our anxiety and rest in the Lord.

The first encouragement in Psalm 39 is found in the vastness of God. The psalmist describes how small he feels in verses 4 and 5, reminding us how brief is our life in comparison to a God who has always been and always will be. Like a child caught in the embrace of a loving parent, there is security in knowing that even though our "lifetime is as nothing in [God's] sight" our God still knows the number of hairs on our head.

Second, the psalmist proclaims in verse 7 that our hope is

found in the Lord. Because of the work of Jesus on the cross, we are promised eternal life; an eternity in the reconciled relationship for which we were created. Our hope is found in the fact that no matter how hard or how great the present moments feel, what God still has for us is even greater.

These two encouraging observations invite us to live differently. Instead of cowering in the fear of the inevitable or dreading the end of our lives, we can boldly live in the present because we know that for everything in life there is a season and in the midst of it all, we are truly known. In the vast love of God and the assurance of Jesus Christ, we can move from fear to freedom.

Blessing

May you know that the God who created you and sent you into the world already knows when you will return. May you never live in fear, but live boldly and richly in community with Christ and others until the very end. May you find hope in the vastness of God and the truth that you are known. May you live fully into each season as it comes, and embrace all the Lord has to teach you.

Reflection

What do you fear? How can you find freedom from that fear in Christ?

Psalm 40

1 I waited patiently for the Lord;
   he inclined to me and heard my cry.

2 He drew me up from the desolate pit,
   out of the miry bog,
   and set my feet upon a rock,
   making my steps secure.

3 He put a new song in my mouth,
   a song of praise to our God.
   Many will see and fear,
   and put their trust in the Lord...

6 Sacrifice and offering you do not desire,
   but you have given me an open ear.
   Burnt offering and sin offering
   you have not required.

7 Then I said, "Here I am;
   in the scroll of the book it is written of me.

8 I delight to do your will, O my God;
   your law is within my heart."

Truth

Every time I read or sing these words from Psalm 40, I'm struck by the image of God, Creator of the universe, all-powerful, all-knowing, with no need for humanity, condescending and reaching down to our human level into the pit, a miry bog, to carry us out to solid ground. It's an incredible image and so wholly other than the gods of the ancient near eastern world. Other gods of the time needed worshipers to offer sacrifice and they needed to be worshiped. God has no need for humans, yet constantly draws us out of the depths of our sins because God desires relationship with us; God protects us and saves us and makes our footing sure on solid ground as we move through life. There is no other god like our God.

David goes on to speak of burnt and sin offerings, a further comparison to the pagan gods of the ancient culture. The important thing to keep in mind here is that God didn't require animal sacrifice to be appeased of some kind of bloodlust like the sacrifice practiced in the worship of pagan gods of the time. Instead, God repurposed a pagan practice as an act of mercy. Animal sacrifice wasn't how God felt worshiped; rather, it allowed God's people to worship. God hears us with an open ear without the ritual of sacrifice because God is like no other. We see the words echoed back in Hebrews as God sent a final sacrifice, Jesus, to make clear that what God truly desires is restoration and relationship.

God isn't interested in current cultural whims, but rather, God's character holds true and is always seeking reconciliation and wholeness for the world, for you, for your children, and for me. No matter the hardship in which we find ourselves, may we cling to the hope found in this truth: God doesn't need us but chooses us anyway.

Blessing

May you cry out to God for help and safety in all things, trusting and knowing that God cares for you. May you live your days with a song of praise on your lips as you remember the ways in which God has delivered you and protected you.

Reflection

Have you ever had an experience where you felt like God was physically carrying you out of a pit? Do you trust God enough to cry out in times of utter despair?

Psalm 41

1 Happy are those who consider the poor;
   the Lord delivers them in the day of trouble.

2 The Lord protects them and keeps them alive;
   they are called happy in the land.
   You do not give them up to the will of their enemies.

3 The Lord sustains them on their sickbed;
   in their illness you heal all their infirmities.

Trust

Sickness is pervasive in our lives. Whether it's the season for a perpetually runny nose, which always seems to happen around our home during the colder months, or something much more serious that has us up in the middle of the night making a trip to the hospital, the psalmist is commenting on a very familiar reality in Psalm 41. The encouragement we find in this psalm is linked to the truth that God sees our sickness and is present in our time of need.

In order to get the most out of this passage, quite a bit of unpacking of verse 1 is needed. First, the word "Happy" is the same word as the very first word in Psalm 1:1, which means "blessed". Second, "consider" here means more than merely thinking about, it means truly gaining wisdom from. Finally, "the poor" references those who are poor in health, weak, or helpless. The reason this is important is because verse 1 is saying that those who understand and are aware of the ways God cares for the sick will find rest and encouragement.

When we look to the testimony of others and learn from the ways that God has sustained, delivered, and healed them, we are encouraged because we can know that the same will be true for the loved ones in our lives. Does this mean that all Christians who are sick will find physical healing this side of heaven? No, but it does mean that God is for the poor and infirm and promises to deliver us. Ecclesiastes 3:1 says, "for every time there is a season..." which means that there are seasons of sickness, seasons of health, seasons of life, and seasons of death, but God promises to always stick with us through it all and in Jesus, we have the promise of renewed life, both now and forevermore.

Blessing

Little one, in life there are seasons for all things and it is only in embracing the easy and the difficult that we experience the fullness of life. When times get tough, may you know that God is always with you. May you know the healing power of Jesus Christ in your life and may you intimately feel the Holy Spirit's presence as God cares for you and keeps you forever close.

Reflection

What lessons have you learned from the harder seasons of sickness, death, mourning, and loss in your life?

Psalm 42

1 As a deer longs for flowing streams,
   so my soul longs for you, O God.

2 My soul thirsts for God,
   for the living God.
  When shall I come and behold
   the face of God?

3 My tears have been my food
   day and night,
  while people say to me continually,
   "Where is your God?"

4 These things I remember,
   as I pour out my soul:
  how I went with the throng,
   and led them in procession to the house of God,
  with glad shouts and songs of thanksgiving,
   a multitude keeping festival.

5 Why are you cast down, O my soul,
   and why are you disquieted within me?
  Hope in God; for I shall again praise him,
   my help

Truth

We've all experienced some level of thirst. Though it's difficult for me to imagine the degree of thirst of someone who has gone days without drink, I can still call to mind the feeling of the first sip of cold water when I've been outside on a hot day. That desire for water to quench a parched throat becomes all-consuming. The only thought is that crisp, cold drink. Imagine how all-consuming this would be for someone who has gone much longer without water.

Can you imagine longing for God in this same way? It's easy to not rely on God in our culture (at least temporarily). Our world is so much different from the psalmist's; so many of our basic needs are met, and we can distract ourselves with media and consumerism to the point where our "thirst" has been quenched and we don't have to think about our sorrow or our pain. Though, of course, that is a fleeting solution, and so we reach again and again for immediate tangible gratification instead of seeking the one who can truly quench our deepest thirst.

I love this next section of the psalm. It's such a powerful image of faith to me. The psalmist is longing for God and feels that God is far away. Yet instead of wallowing in despair, the psalmist calls to mind times when he was full of praise and thanksgiving, when God felt near and it was impossible not to praise God. The psalmist roots his hope in that memory, knowing that he will praise God again and that God will carry him through this hardship, quenching his thirst and sustaining him through the night. That is true reliance and the only way to true satisfaction.

Blessing

May you praise God with thanksgiving and gladness and always remember the ways in which God has carried you and protected you in times of trouble. May you hold to the hope that the God who has delivered you and brought you gladness will do it again and again.

Reflection

What earthly things do you reach for to soothe yourself before going to God with your troubles? Like the psalmist, do you recall better times and past times of praise when you are feeling far from God?

Psalm 43

5 Why are you cast down, O my soul,
  and why are you disquieted within me?

Truth

Sometimes it's the little questions in the Psalms that speak most clearly. When I read the above question, I had to pause and evaluate. Have you had a moment like this?

For me, there are two main circumstances which often lead to me asking the psalmist's question. The first is when I am overwhelmed. I tend to be a person who likes to take huge bites out of all that life offers. My wife jokes that I make a hobby out of starting new things–implying that I often don't finish what I begin. I tend to make a lot of commitments that inevitably begin to encroach on one another, leaving me short on time and exhausted. While I have been significantly working on this over the last couple of years, I still quite often find my soul warning me that I am overwhelmed. Whether it's due to distress, frustration, or just busyness, my soul becomes cast down when I am overwhelmed.

The second circumstance is a bit harder to pin down. The disquiet of my soul can be jarring and seem to come out of nowhere. I will go to bed feeling on top of the world and when I rise in the morning, something is just off. It's in these moments that my soul is in tension with my thoughts and the only thing I can do is stop, slow down, and listen.

The truth is that whatever reason on the surface has caused disquiet, the underlying reason is tied to our soul's thirst for God. Whether we become too busy, over-committed, and overwhelmed, or whether we drift away because everything in life seems to be going great, our soul knows that we need to be connected to the Source of life. In Psalm 43, the psalmist is in trouble and needs help from God and after calling out, is met with hope. The reason that the psalmist feels so confident in calling out to God is because he has his priorities straight. Our souls are a great barometer for our priorities, so be sure to take account often and remember that when we put God first, we drink deeply from the Source of life, which then overflows in everything else we do. Prioritize the Source.

Blessing

May you always prioritize your relationship with God above all else. But, when life distracts or dismays you, may your soul redirect you to the true source of life, Jesus Christ.

Reflection

When was the last time that you asked the same question as the psalmist?

May They Be Blessed

Psalm 44

8 In God we have boasted continually,
*   and we will give thanks to your name forever. Selah*

9 Yet you have rejected us and abased us,
*   and have not gone out with our armies.*

10 You made us turn back from the foe,
*   and our enemies have gotten spoil.*

11 You have made us like sheep for slaughter,
*   and have scattered us among the nations.*

12 You have sold your people for a trifle,
*   demanding no high price for them.*

13 You have made us the taunt of our neighbors,
*   the derision and scorn of those around us.*

14 You have made us a byword among the nations,
*   a laughingstock among the peoples.*

Truth

This psalm is difficult to sit with; the desperation, the frustration, and the anger. The emotions that the psalmist expresses in this passage is palpable. It's a lament one can find throughout all of scripture. Why do you ignore your people, God? Why do you let us be defeated, taken from the land, and humiliated when all we want to do is proclaim your name to the nations? This is what the psalmist is asking after describing the way his army trusted not in their own weapons but in the strength of God, and yet still lost. It's a natural path for the human mind to take. It's extremely difficult to imagine our own existence as a blip in the story of human history, and it's impossible to understand the ways in which God works as Creator and keeper of the entire universe.

Even now, we look to the news and hear stories of Christians around the world facing death and humiliation, we can see on a day-to-day basis the apparent triumph of evil over good as corrupt regimes rise, and truth and justice fall. It's disheartening, and the truth is that though our lives are a small part of the story of humanity, it's still our reality that our day-to-day hours are spent crying out to God to do something. Pushing into this frustration is vital to true intimacy with God. If we don't seek to understand, if we don't continually call to God to act, even when we don't understand how or when God will do it, we're not seeking to learn more about our Creator. Ultimately, we're left with the truth of scripture that God is vast and mysterious and not fully knowable to human minds, but we're also given the truth, the unbreakable promise, that God's plan is to redeem and restore. The days might be hard, and there will be times when we see evil prevail, but it is a temporary victory. This is not how God's story ends. The Kingdom of God will reign on earth, and all evil will be destroyed.

Blessing

May you press into relationship with God always, seeking to know more fully the depth of God's love, compassion, and heart for justice in the world. May you come to God with the fullness of your frustration, while keeping your hope anchored in the Kingdom yet to come.

Reflection

Do you relate to the anger that the psalmist expresses here? How can you fix your eyes on the coming promises of God while seeking to know God's heart more fully?

Psalm 45

1 My heart overflows with a goodly theme;
   I address my verses to the king;
   my tongue is like the pen of a ready scribe.

2 You are the most handsome of men;
   grace is poured upon your lips;
   therefore God has blessed you forever.

6 Your throne, O God, endures forever and ever.
   Your royal scepter is a scepter of equity;

7 you love righteousness and hate wickedness.
   Therefore God, your God, has anointed you
   with the oil of gladness beyond your companions;

8 your robes are all fragrant with myrrh and aloes and cassia.

Truth

In its original context, this psalm was thought to have been written in celebration of a royal wedding and it appears that this marriage may have ushered in the rule of a new king. This psalm praises the qualities of the new king, declares a blessing over the marriage, and points out God's faithfulness. However, as we know from Israel's history, the quality of their kings varied significantly from one generation to the next and even the most praised king, King David, was a sinful and often selfish individual. So while this text was written about a person who was crowned king, the Church has historically reinterpreted this text to be a description of the one true king, King Jesus. Let's take a look at two key things that this psalm proclaims about Jesus.

Verse 2, written about Jesus, reminds us that Jesus was a perfect exemplar of humanity. While "handsome" typically connotes beauty, a better understanding of "most handsome" for this context is that Jesus is the epitome of humanity. It's important to remember that when God took on human flesh, humanity was reconciled back into relationship with God. Since Jesus was one hundred percent divine and one hundred percent human, all that Jesus did on earth, God was inherently doing as well. Verse 2 reminds us that Jesus lived an exemplary life that modeled the life we are called to emulate as Christians.

Second, verses 6-8 show that Jesus is anointed by God to carry out acts that are in line with God's heart, equitable acts of mercy and justice. In calling His disciples and His followers to righteousness, Jesus proclaimed the love of God and embodied it in the way He lived. He cared for the ostracised and the marginalized. He ate with tax collectors and stood up for adulterers. Jesus did everything out of the love of God and asked His followers to do the same. "I give you a new commandment, that you love one another. Just as I have loved you, you also should love one another. By this everyone will know that you are my disciples, if you have love for one another" (John 13:34-35).

Blessing

May you be inspired by the example of Christ. May you know that you too have been anointed through the power of the Holy Spirit to live like Jesus and bring hope and love to our world. And may you know that Jesus came, lived, and died for you so that you could be in intimate relationship with God.

Reflection

Grace pours from the lips of Christ, do you receive that in your own life? Do you extend the same to others? How can you do both better?

Psalm 46

1 God is our refuge and strength,
   a very present help in trouble.

2 Therefore we will not fear, though the earth should change,
   though the mountains shake in the heart of the sea;

3 though its waters roar and foam,
   though the mountains tremble with its tumult. Selah

4 There is a river whose streams make glad the city of God,
   the holy habitation of the Most High.

5 God is in the midst of the city; it shall not be moved;
   God will help it when the morning dawns.

6 The nations are in an uproar, the kingdoms totter;
   he utters his voice, the earth melts.

7 The Lord of hosts is with us;
   the God of Jacob is our refuge.

Truth

This psalm is one of those passages that I repeat to myself, almost like a mantra. The truth is so tangible, so full of hope, and it's a summation of who God is. It's a truth that sustains us and helps us remember that nothing on earth is out of God's control and power. It's the type of truth that places my troubles in perspective and fixes my eyes on the end-goal, the coming Kingdom and the redemption of all of creation to God. We do not toil in vain, and I need reminding of this often. God is present in all that we experience, and no matter what changes on earth, no matter what disasters, tragedies, wars, regimes, or laws, God is present and God's Kingdom is coming. It is here and its fulfillment is yet to come. I just let out a sigh of relief as I wrote those words. This is something I need to remind myself of every day.

God is in the midst of the city, the holy city that will not be moved. God's plan for redemption has not and will not change. God is bringing the Kingdom no matter how humanity tries to get in the way or deny the inevitable. And even when we war with each other, seek power instead of godliness and strive after the wrong things, the earth and all of its inhabitants still rest in the hands of God–the earth melts at the sound of God's voice. As God's people, it's too easy to look at the world and drown in despair. We are so far off from God's plan, but we can rest in the truth that God is with us. We are invited to partner with God in the plan for humanity's redemption, and it will still happen no matter the ways we fall short.

Blessing

May you cling to God's presence in times of trouble, trusting in God to be your refuge and strength and in the coming hope of the Kingdom. May you glimpse God's Kingdom here and now while still fixing your eyes on all that God will yet do.

Reflection

Does this passage help you put the sin of the world in perspective? Can you still trust that God commands the earth even when you see so much evil and darkness within it?

Psalm 47

5 God has gone up with a shout,
  the Lord with the sound of a trumpet.

6 Sing praises to God, sing praises;
  sing praises to our King, sing praises.

7 For God is the king of all the earth;
  sing praises with a psalm.

8 God is king over the nations;
  God sits on his holy throne.

9 The princes of the peoples gather
  as the people of the God of Abraham.
  For the shields of the earth belong to God;
  he is highly exalted.

Truth

Psalm 47 is the epitome of a praise psalm through and through. It serves as a reminder, an instruction, an encouragement, and a liturgy for the community of God, both for its original context and for us still today. The root praise is found in verse 8. God's people praise because God is the king over all nations. This is true. However, it is important that we unpack this idea carefully so that we don't fall into the same trap of religious triumphalism that the Jewish religious elite were guilty of in the New Testament.

The danger comes from the line of thought that any one group of people is more important, more loved, or more highly valued than another. It's tempting to believe that the chosen nature of God's people is exclusive. Those in the club are blessed, while those on the outside are not. However, in Jesus, we see that the love of God is radically inclusive, because Jesus is drawing all of creation back into a redeemed relationship with God. When we look at the entire story of the Bible, we see that God always intended for all of humanity to be equally cared for, seen, and loved. God chose Israel first to be an example of and to testify to what God can do in the lives of those who follow God. God blessed Israel so that the world could see the love that God has for everyone.

The bottom line is that God is the God of all humanity, not because God's power makes it so, but because God's love for us all runs so deep and wide and long and high that through Jesus God has made a place for us all in God's kingdom.

Blessing

May you always remember that you are deeply loved, beautifully unique, and intentionally made. May you be inspired to live into your identity as a chosen child of God and may you remember to share the truth that your God loves and cares for all people equally.

Reflection

In what ways have you seen the church struggle with religious triumphalism?

Psalm 48

9 We ponder your steadfast love, O God,
 in the midst of your temple.

10 Your name, O God, like your praise,
 reaches to the ends of the earth.
 Your right hand is filled with victory.

11 Let Mount Zion be glad,
 let the towns[a] of Judah rejoice
 because of your judgments.

12 Walk about Zion, go all around it,
 count its towers,

13 consider well its ramparts;
 go through its citadels,
 that you may tell the next generation

14 that this is God,
 our God forever and ever.
 He will be our guide forever.

Truth

It can be difficult to understand the significance of the temple and the nations' response to God and God's people because of it, due to it being an idea that is so far removed from our current context. The temple was the meeting place for God and God's people, the place where heaven and earth intersected, the place where God was able to dwell with God's people. This changes because of Jesus. Just as the temple was once an earthly symbol of God's love and strength and dominion over earth, so too is the story and person of Jesus. Modern Christians can point to His life, death and resurrection as a demonstration of the strength and power of God and God's dominion over death and sin.

It was impossible for the people of God to look upon the temple without praise on their lips. It was impossible for God's enemies to see its grand structure and not recognize their inferiority. The people of the ancient world filled God's temple with praise, and we too can be a part of that legacy, lifting our praise in the name of Jesus, as God's enemies on earth tremble before the power of Jesus and all that He came to proclaim. The generations before us and those that will come after can look to the scriptures, the faith of the Hebrew people, the work of Jesus, the image of the temple now embodied through the Holy Spirit living in each of us, and see that God will guide the faithful, delivering them and reconciling them forever and ever.

Blessing

May you dwell in sacred spaces, filling the earth with praise for God, and see glimpses of heaven on earth. May you proclaim and reflect the work of Christ, so that the light and love of God shines from you, a testament to the legacy of God's faithful people.

Reflection

In 1 Corinthians 6:19 Paul says "your body is a temple of the Holy Spirit" because the Holy Spirit lives in us now. How does this change the way you think about God's temple?

Psalm 49

16 Do not be afraid when some become rich,
   when the wealth of their houses increases.

17 For when they die they will carry nothing away;
   their wealth will not go down after them.

18 Though in their lifetime they count themselves happy
   —for you are praised when you do well for yourself—

19 they will go to the company of their ancestors,
   who will never again see the light.

Truth

Money is a pervasive part of our culture. It is the way in which the majority of us put food on our tables and provide comfort and security for our families. Money and wealth, even being considered to be a rich person, are not bad nor are they sinful. It's true that our relationship with money is a bit different in the 21st century than it was back when the wisdom of this psalm was being circulated amongst the Israelite people. However, this psalm still contains a lesson that is very applicable for us today.

The psalmist simply makes the point that money is a tool and not a means toward salvation. This may seem obvious–everyone knows you can't buy eternal salvation or reconciliation with God. But the psalmist's message is more nuanced than that. The psalmist's point is that if we aren't careful, we will prioritize money, wealth, and comfort over our relationship with God. Similar to the story of the rich young ruler in the New Testament, Jesus asks us to set aside the things of this world, so that we can fully live into the life for which God created us. The majority of us aren't called to liquidate our assets and give away all of our cash. However, just like the rich young ruler, each of us is called to set aside the things that stand between us and Christ and make our relationship with God first priority.

In our culture, upward mobility, materialism, and status are praised, which means that unless we teach our children to see money as a tool and an opportunity for generosity, the culture will teach them the wrong message.

Blessing

May you always put Jesus Christ first in your life and recognize that all the worldly things are fleeting. May you never be afraid of or controlled by wealth, but rather may you see the ways you can use it to care for yourself and for others. May you recognize the many blessings in your life for what they are–opportunities to mirror the character of your Creator and share abundantly with others.

Reflection

How is your relationship with money? How do you want your child's relationship with money to be?

Psalm 50

3 *Our God comes and does not keep silence,*
  before him is a devouring fire,
  and a mighty tempest all around him...

7 *"Hear, O my people, and I will speak,*
  O Israel, I will testify against you.
  I am God, your God.

8 *Not for your sacrifices do I rebuke you;*
  your burnt offerings are continually before me...

14 *Offer to God a sacrifice of thanksgiving,*
   and pay your vows to the Most High.

15 *Call on me in the day of trouble;*
   I will deliver you, and you shall glorify me.

Truth

The poetry of the book of Psalms is rich with the legacy of Israel's people. The opening of this psalm talks about a devouring fire and a mighty tempest all around God. To the original audience, this imagery would have been a clear reference to the exodus story and the wandering of God's people in the wilderness. It was the mighty tempest that God used to defeat the Egyptians and allow the children of Israel to escape. Then God was present with the people through a pillar of fire as they traveled. Despite having a rich faith legacy and being given chance after chance to live up to the covenant God made with the Israelites, they slipped repeatedly into idol worship, sin, and separation from God. The psalmists calls them to remember God's past faithfulness in order to persevere in their current faith journey.

It's so easy to get caught up in the motions of faith and lose touch with our active relationship and covenant with God. This has always been a struggle for God's people. Those motions of belief can look like showing up to church, singing the songs, smiling through a sermon, and for the ancient Israelites, it looked like offering sacrifices to God but withholding the allegiance of their hearts. The psalmist makes clear that God doesn't want empty offerings, only pious actions. God wants our hearts and our thanksgiving. If we are to truly live a life faithful to our Creator God, it looks less like performing the right rituals and more like calling on God in times of trouble, a true reliance on God and pursuing a relationship of intimacy with and glorying in the One through whom all creation exists.

Whether we like it or not, our kids are watching all the ways we live out our faith and they can discern the posture of our hearts. While it's our job to pass on the stories of faith and be a witness to our kids of the ways God is working in our lives, we also must remember that what is in our hearts sometimes speaks louder than our actions, and a life lived out of a place of dwelling with God is the perfect example of what we hope our kids adopt in their own faith journey with Christ.

Blessing

May you always remember the ways that God has been faithful in your life and in the life of your family. May you seek God fully with your heart and mind, not in your actions alone. And may you always seek to see God's heart behind the calling and instruction in your life.

Reflection

The act of remembrance in order to continue in faithful devotion to God is seen all over Scripture, just like in this psalm. When God feels far from you, do you recall past stories of God's deliverance and faithfulness?

Acknowledgments

Books like this don't write themselves and writers don't get to write if they don't have an amazing support system. So here is a thank you to all of the people that have supported us in one way or another.

While we could fill a whole book with the names of our supporters, teachers, friends, and family. A few specific people have to be named.

First, our spouses. Matt and Emily it's impossible to describe in a finite space your infinite love and support for us. Thank you for showing up everyday, we are better people because of you.

Second, a huge thanks goes out to Joey McFeron, our Editor. Thank you for seamlessly integrating our work and unifying our voices, for making sure we clearly communicated our points, and for helping us to stick to the vision of this book when we might have otherwise gone astray. The final polish is all thanks to you.

Finally, thank you to those whose financial contributions through Patreon made this book and the continual ministry of Constant Source possible.

Constant Source

reimaging family discipleship

For More Content

Please Visit Our Website

www.theconstantsource.com